East of Eden

East of Eden

SPIRITUAL REFLECTIONS ON REPENTANT FOLLOWING

TALBERT O. SHAW

THE PILGRIM PRESS

CLEVELAND

Dedication

TO MY PARENTS,

the late Albert and Albertha Shaw,

who instilled within me the vision, hope,

and spiritual stamina to pursue, relentlessly,

the journey East of Eden.

The Pilgrim Press, 700 Prospect Avenue, Cleveland, Ohio 44115-1100
pilgrimpress.com
© 2003 by Talbert O. Shaw

Unless otherwise noted, biblical quotations are from the New Revised
Standard Version of the Bible © copyright 1989 by the Division of Christian
Education of the National Council of the Churches of Christ in the U.S.A.,
and are used by permission.

Printed in the United States of America on acid-free paper

08   07   06   05   04   03   5   4   3   2   1

Library of Congress Cataloging-in-Publication Data

Shaw, Talbert O.
     East of Eden : spiritual reflections on repentant following / Talbert O.
Shaw.
         p. cm.
     Includes bibliographical references.
     ISBN 0-8298-1565-1 (pbk. : alk. paper)
     1. Sin. 2. Good and evil. 3. Repentance. 4. Christian life. I. Title.

BT715.S46   2003
234'.5—dc22
                                                           2003059666

CONTENTS

FOREWORD

IN *East of Eden,* Talbert Shaw has parted from the path of popularity to deal with themes related to human alienation and sin. He starts with the predicament of a humanity driven eastward out of the Eden of primeval innocence. While he never stops short of a word of hope, his commentary on the human condition is candidly penetrating and inescapably relevant. And all of this is accomplished in a writing style graced with easy flow and eloquent language.

The theme of human sin was over-emphasized and dramatized almost a century ago by preachers like Billy Sunday with a resulting backlash in much of the popular mind. Dr. Shaw has avoided the stereotypical extremes of negativity that once prevailed and has graciously and readably confronted the human foibles that still need to be confessed and cleansed.

This theologically inclined ethicist is also an artist, painting unforgettable, vivid portraits and realistic scenes. His scholarly supply of details is naturally presented in low-profile, eye-witness quality accounts. They supply a rich reservoir for readers who happen also to be laden with the task of preaching every Sunday.

Perhaps most importantly, these messages are profoundly insightful, opening up the Bible with surprisingly fresh and meaningful angles of vision. One is often made to wonder, "Now why didn't I see that detail or that meaning when I first read about that boy with the fishes and loaves, or that compassionate Samaritan?" Perhaps Dr. Shaw's habits of spotting these fascinating items can be acquired by looking at and living into the scenes he saw, rather than scanning scriptures for clever, abstract ideas.

We are indebted to Talbert Shaw for his creative and candid exploration of this all-too-overlooked territory East of Eden.

—*Henry H. Mitchell*

ACKNOWLEDGEMENTS

CONTRIBUTORS TO THIS CRYSTALLIZATION of my spiritual journey include those teachers in college and seminary who saw in me a diamond in the rough. Too numerous to name, they remain my unsung heroes. I must, however, thank my wife, Marlene, whose patience and support remained unabated as I juggled the hours between writing and leading a university.

Particular gratitude goes to Mrs. Marilyn Fields, my administrative assistant, who found the time to type the manuscript through numerous revisions without a tinge of protest.

Finally, I would like to thank my children, who seemed to keep focus despite my long hours away from home.

INTRODUCTION

THIS BOOK OF SPIRITUAL REFLECTIONS crystallizes my personal quest for spiritual maturation, as well as more than fifty years of prophetic preaching. Thus, it represents both a testimony and a testament.

A testimony of a dying man preaching the gospel to dying men and women seeking hope and promise. For a preacher must adhere to the Pauline exhortation, "Therefore, my beloved, just as you have always obeyed me, not only in my presence, but much more now in my absence, work out your own salvation with fear and trembling" (Phil. 2:12).

But these spiritual reflections are also a testament, an evidence and proof, a declaration of the hope that is in me punctuated by five decades of preaching. I have seen travail of souls as believers struggle to overcome fear and doubt. I have heard the struggling faith say, "God, why me?" after a personal tragedy.

Some even ask, "Where is God?" a question posing both belief and disappointment. So the following of faith is a "sympathetic antipathy" (Kierkegaard) drawn by belief and repelled by doubt. Jesus met a man with this tensional paradox. "I believe; help my unbelief!" (Mark 9:24). Doesn't this speak of the human experience?

Human nature presupposes bouts of uncertainty and doubt in the business of living. Reinhold Neibuhr, one of America's most distinguished ethicists, in his excellent analysis of human nature delineates the irresolvable conflict between the physical and spiritual nature of human beings. Tied inexorably to physical limitations and physical needs (hunger, thirst, self-preservation, sexual desires, self-interests, etc.) but possessing the capacity of self-transcendence by way of the spirit, human beings encounter inevitable conflicts in pragmatic decisions. The spirit may reach for lofty ideals, such as altruism, but nature, the physical aspect of our being, demands that each decision also preserves self-interest.[1] Every action involves conflict between nature and spirit. So every action, despite its altruistic intent, is tainted with self-interest.

Accordingly, there is inevitable tension between altruism and personal interest, a conflict that has religious implications. The Apostle Paul echoes this conflict existentially, "For I do not do the good I want, but the evil I do not want is what I do" (Rom. 7:19). Here, Paul speaks as a believer, a Christian, and a preacher. Conversion into a believer does not resolve the paradox—the conflict between nature and spirit—usually conceived as war between the flesh and spirit. It accentuates the need for a power beyond the self. Hope resides in a Savior who is not impeded by human limitations.

Predisposition to this paradox, this universal human experience called by some original sin, defines precisely the human condition. So potent, pervasive, and determinative of human behavior, Paul calls it the war between good and evil. Evil seems always to win, but there is hope, a hope driven by faith in Christ. Paul says, "Wretched man that I am! Who will rescue me from the body of death? Thanks be to God through Jesus Christ our Lord!" (Rom. 7:24–25).

Informed by this paradox—this contradiction in human nature that inevitably influences human behavior, thus raising serious ethical questions of right and wrong—these spiritual reflections summon us to act faithfully and bravely and leave ultimate judgment to God. For act we must. But acts of faith intend the good of neighbor; thus they are blameless, if not always harmless. In this spirit, St. Augustine advises the faithful to love God and to do what you want. This is no libertarian ethic unconcerned with appropriate means and legitimate ends. Augustine is not an advocate of ethical anomy. His starting point is the love of God, and as a guiding principle, true love of God constrains from evil motives and destructive ends. Such love engenders commitment to the common good.[2]

It is crucial to be mindful of human imperfection, however devoid of ultimate certainty, while we act faithfully and bravely. There is no such thing as perfect faith. Scripture defines human beings as broken vessels, and as the humans of the Bible, our prayer should be, "God, I believe. Help my unbelief." Contradiction in human nature, the state of human imperfection—belief tainted with unbelief—all define our status as "reluctant converts." Reluctant means lack of ultimate certainty and the need for daily renewal; thus arises the relentless quest for certainty. The journey of faith may be appropriately defined as "repentant following," for only constant, continual contact with the Author and Finisher of faith will enliven the limping, lingering, and at times, the languishing state of belief.

If this picture of the Christian pilgrimage seems to engender despair and fear, because of the contradictions in human nature and the lack of ultimate certainty, the apostle Paul brings a message predicated on hope. He exhorts, "For in hope we were saved. Now hope that is seen is not hope. For who hopes for what is seen?" (Rom. 8:24). This is the conclusion of the dialectic between nature and spirit with all the attendant ethical questions. Humans are invested with the critical capacity to hope in God's saving promises. Humanity's capacity to hope makes salvation possible; but humanity's inclination to doubt makes hope necessary. Yes, we are saved by hope. Human ingenuity can invent no other way. Thanks be to God who gives faith the victory.

PART ONE

The Human Condition

One

EAST OF EDEN

Therefore the Lord God sent him forth
from the garden of Eden, to till the ground from
which he was taken. He drove out the man;
and at the east of the garden of Eden he placed the
cherubim, and a sword flaming and turning
to guard the way to the tree of life.

—Genesis 3:23–24

A YOUNG MAN DEPLANED in Montego Bay, Jamaica, after a short flight from his homeland in the United States of America, dropped to his knees, and kissed the ground declaring, "Thank you, God, for this island paradise." Jamaica, for this young man, with its gleaming white sands, aquamarine blue sea, bright sunshine, waterfalls, and verdant mountains populated by a fun-loving people, is the equivalent of paradise. But sand, sea, and sun do not constitute the paradise from which Adam was driven. Paradise means wholeness and harmony, characteristics that are absent from human relations all over planet Earth. This state of brokenness in social relations exists because life on this planet is lived east of Eden.

Earth's tragic and ambiguous pilgrimage begins with the Genesis account of Adam's expulsion from paradise. It describes God's "strange act," separating the first family from idyllic conditions, conditions accentuated by harmony. The third chapter of Genesis delineates four harmonic relations in Eden. First, a harmony between God and humanity, for there were daily conversations between humankind and the Creator. There existed psychological harmony as

· 1 ·

Adam and Eve enjoyed guiltless blissful glee, surrounded by everything that hearts could desire. Social/familial concord adorned relations in Eden as its inhabitants obeyed and worshipped in unison. Even nature, animals, trees, and soil produced in abundance while contributing to this pristine, unspoiled comprehensive, homeostatic environment called Eden.

Clearly, theological, psychological, social, and environmental harmonies are irreplaceable ingredients in a place called paradise. Their absence is the place named East of Eden. The text before us declares that Adam and Eve listened to another voice, a voice that offered improvement on God's plan. Evaluating the creation, Genesis declares, "God saw everything that he had made, and indeed, it was very good. And there was evening and there was morning, the sixth day" (Gen. 1:31). But it was not good enough for humankind's inquisitive appetite. Evil, catastrophe, brokenness await disobedience. Ecclesiastes states, "See, this alone I found, that God made human beings straightforward, but they have devised many schemes" (Eccl. 7:29).

One such invention was dissatisfaction with one's created state, one's state of finitude. Adam and Eve wanted to be as "god." Their eyes were opened, but to evil and disobedience; innocence disappeared, nakedness ensued, fig leaves replaced God's righteousness, and separation, brokenness, progressive deterioration, and eventually death took over God's creation. Disharmonies could not exist in paradise, and since humankind was the source of this evil, Adam and Eve were driven out of the garden to East of Eden.

East of Eden is everything that paradise is not. Paradise is unspoiled, pristine, comprehensive harmony among God, humankind, and animals. Even the earth contributes to this idyllic nature of things. Four harmonies are broken. Adam hides from God among the trees; he blames Eve for leading him into disobedience; guilt replaces innocence, thus the onset of psychological eccentricities; Eve blames the tempter, and earth brings forth "thorns and thistles." Theological, social/familial, psychological, and environmental brokenness are the characteristics of our home called East of Eden through the ages.

Chaos, social anomy, humans' inhumanity to humans, the blot on human history called slavery, destructive wars among nations, spousal abuse, abuse of children, various forms of injustices, ethnic hatred, drug abuse, and every conceivable evil among humans are attributable to theological, social, psychological, and environmental brokenness on our planet. The rape of nature, called willful pollution by some, is evidence of lack of appreciation for the source of our physical health and well-being.

Of all the pathologies and pain experienced by humans this side of Eden, none is more devastating than those occurring in human relations. This real story is typical. It appeared in the *Washington Star* on 18 July 1977. Bob and Pauline Drummond became foster parents to a newborn boy named Timmy, the product of two young people who gave him up for adoption. For two and a half years, Bob and Pauline poured love and quality care on little Timmy. Bonding between these foster parents and Timmy achieved such intensity that adoption was pursued. Bob and Pauline felt such great love for Timmy that they began to see him as their own.

What the Drummonds, who are white, didn't know was that Timmy was the child of a 17-year-old white girl and a young black man. After four months, Timmy's mixed race became obvious. His complexion turned olive, his hair turned curly. Neighbors, East of Eden dwellers, began asking questions regarding the child's ethnicity. A problem now faced the Drummonds and the Fulton County Department of Family Services in Georgia. Recall, if you will, that in East of Eden it is legally prohibited for white couples to adopt children of black parents. As products of this culture of prejudice, the Drummonds admitted that they probably would not have thought of adopting Timmy had they known that he was biracial. But attitudinal changes can take place in this chaotic world. After loving and caring for Timmy and now seeing him as their "own," the Drummonds stated, "We probably would have reacted differently twenty years ago, but we have changed for the better. Those people who believe that there will be separate stalls in heaven for blacks and whites will be sadly mistaken. You can't help but love a boy you have raised for two and a half years and who has called you mommy and daddy—as hard as folks find it to believe. Why is this so hard to get over?"

But the State of Georgia was against this effort by the Drummonds despite their plea and the recommendation of Timmy's natural mother that the adoption proceed. To plead their case, the Drummonds moved to a new neighborhood and enlarged their home by adding a new room for Timmy. The State of Georgia raised questions about Pauline's health, but the hospital declared her in perfect health. Social workers questioned her ability to raise a child from a different culture, and the Drummonds offered to study black history.

Against recommendations by a social worker, the natural parents, and a psychologist that removal of Timmy from his psychological parents would be emotionally traumatic for the child, the Georgia court ruled against the adoption. Timmy was pulled from Pauline's caring hands, screaming as he left court into a new unknown world. With tears streaming down her cheeks, Mrs. Drummond said, "I hope Timmy will get lots of love and attention." In response to later inquiries regarding him, she was told, "Timmy is no longer crying for you."

Oh yes, in East of Eden, injustice and prejudice still reign. There are little Timmys crying all over the world. Is there any question why there is the relentless search for Utopia, this no place, this place of bliss and harmony? But there is hope, for triumph and tragedy can coexist in our world.

Short of paradise restored, human existence is sentenced to the contradictions and paradoxes consistent with the fractured relations in East of Eden. Believers, the Church, are sent into the world to live and witness. There is no escape from the need to live faithfully and make tough personal and social decisions in this business of living. Some have sought for Utopia here, but this word "utopia" means no place. It remains a figment of humankind's fertile imagination, triggered by a sense of memory and hope. And we are saved by hope.

There is hope. Abraham, the father of the faithful, served God East of Eden. David, the friend of God, ruled East of Eden. Job, the afflicted, persevered in East of Eden. Jeremiah, the weeping prophet, cried out against evil in East of Eden. Jesus was born, East of Eden. He lived and ministered despite suffering and rejection in this land of shattered relations. Symbols of the crowning redemptive act, the cross, stands east of paradise, defying all the hosts of hell, and the final act in the agelong drama between forces of good and evil will be enacted here. John, the Revelator, declares as he envisions Eden restored, "The kingdom of the world has become the kingdom of our Lord and of his Messiah, and he will reign forever and ever" (Rev. 11:15).

Yes, there is hope this side of Eden. God's "strange act" in expelling disobedience from the garden comes with a promise: "I will put enmity between you and the woman, and between your offspring and hers; he will strike your head, and you will strike his heel" (Gen. 3:15). Bruising the head of evil is lethal; bruising the heel brings persecution and the cross—but with ultimate triumph.

Triumph is promised for faithful following, to those who daily seek to hear the voice of God, the Creator and Redeemer.

All struggle with life's contradictions. Without a hope predicated on some transcendent intervention in human history, what is the future of civilization?

God, send us a ray of hope in this thicket of life that is full of paradoxes and contradictions. Enliven our spirits that we may transcend every hurdle that eventually awaits us East of Eden. Receive our gratitude and praise for the promise of salvation. Amen.

Two

A PERILOUS PAUSE ALONG LIFE'S WAY

Then the Lord said to me:
"You have been skirting this hill country
long enough. Head north...."

—Deuteronomy 2:2–3

CASES OF ABORTED MISSIONS ABOUND. Along life's way there are numerous instances of frustrated dreams, unfulfilled goals, unmet ambitious schemes, and frustrated souls. What began with obvious excitement, copious planning, and plausible goals ended in shoals and shallows, for something happened along the way. Shakespeare informs us that:

> There is a tide in the affairs of men,
> Which, taken at the flood, leads on to fortune;
> Omitted, all the voyage of their life
> Is bound in shallows and in miseries.
> On such a full sea are we now afloat;
> And we must take the current when it serves,
> Or lose our ventures.[3]

I studied with friends in high school and college who conceived ambitious plans for post-college years. Some were brilliant, others less so, but all possessed abilities to achieve their noble objectives. But many swayed as they took the bypass around the required way. Others encamped permanently around some "mountain" incongruous with articulated goals. It's a story of wasted opportunities, stunted talents, lost visions, and, for some, unproductive lives. When applied to discipleship, consequences transcend personal loss; behavior may be construed as blatant disobedience to a divine call or unfaithfulness to a covenant made with God.

The intriguing story of Israel's journey northward from Egypt to Canaan, the promised land, epitomizes the triumphs and tragedies inherent in a pilgrimage of faith. All ingredients in the divine/human encounter on which hinges our salvation appear in this story. There are human enslavement (literal and spiritual), pleas for deliverance by anguished souls, miraculous emancipation, enlightened leadership, recurring temptations along the way, attempted assaults by enemies, divine revelation, blips in leadership, complaints and dissatisfaction by the congregation, relapses into former ways of worship, jealousies among leaders and followers, disobedience, and forgiveness, all transpiring under God's guiding grace and unremitting benevolence. This is the unending drama played out in history and human experience as the agelong struggle between forces of good and evil rages.

As the journey lengthens and disobedience leads into bypasses and unnecessary detours, weariness and tedium tend to vitiate initial excitement. "Why leave Egypt to die in this wilderness?" is the question, spoken and unuttered. When boredom and weariness blur the glorious goal—the promised land—when heightened first-love passion dissipates, when the heart embraces other treasures, then "Entrenched Encampment: Perilous Pauses" displace divinely appointed ends. A vision is vitiated and lost.

At such times, a wake-up call from God is the catalyst to refocus, to renew commitment, and to reenlist in the great and grand procession whose destination is that city whose maker is the great Architect of the Universe. Moses, under divine mandate, issued that clarion call, "You have been skirting this hill country long enough. Head north . . ." (Deut. 2:3). For forty long years Israel meandered in the wilderness sinning, complaining, resisting leadership, reverting to idol worship, and forgetting miraculous delivery from physical and spiritual enslavement. Thirty-eight of those were spent around the southern borders of Canaan, and "many days" around Mount Seir (Deut. 2:1, 7, 14).

"You have been skirting this hill country long enough, head north" comes the divine command with authority and specificity. This entrenched encampment, this perilous pause, this increasing familiar-

ity with "foreigners," this fear of giants all testify of a loss of perspective, unfamiliarity with history, going in the wrong direction.
Head "north," for northward leads home. In this instance, there is no
guessing game, no questioning uncertainty, no need for deductive
logic or philosophical dissertation regarding required behavior.
Specificity accompanies command: "Head north."

Deuteronomy, the fifth book of the Pentateuch (first five books of
the Bible) contains nuggets permanently pertinent to persevering followers. It recapitulates the deliverance, instructions, and expectations
of a people who received special favors from God. It portrays the
profile of a leader, Moses, so devoted to God and committed to his
flock that he begged to be blotted out of the book of life if their sin
could not be forgiven (Ex. 32:32). Here is a shepherd without equal
among mortals.

Years of leadership, forty years, were approaching the end.
Informed that he would not be allowed to lead his flock into Canaan
but must prepare them for entry, Moses, standing this side of Jordan,
delivered four orations, which constitute the Book of Deuteronomy.
These orations stand among the masterpieces of biblical literature.
They are historical, legislative, and hortatory.

To revive a congregation, to regain focus, to stimulate movement
and spiritual maturation, a sense of history is essential. A historical
perspective provides definition, establishes identity, and yields an authoritative basis for the faith within us. "Were you there when . . . ?"
"Yes, I was there when God parted the waters; I ate the manna miraculously provided daily; I saw Moses with the tablets and drank water
from the rock." Reminding Israel of their identity and special place
in God's scheme of things, Moses declared that obedience to God's
commandments and belief in God's promises are prerequisites for
entry into the land of promise.

The orations of Moses were also exhortations to recall and re-
live the mandates of their history. Pride in our roots is necessary and
indeed praiseworthy. Organizational and church connections may
bring prestige, privileges, and power. But although necessary, it is not
sufficient to be of the "seed" of Abraham; one must display his or
her faithfulness and total devotion to God in order to belong to the
family of God.

All who left Egypt with Moses failed to enter Canaan because of disobedience and disbelief. Only their children born along the way and Caleb and Joshua were permitted to enter (Deut. 1:32, 35, 39; 2:16). Entrenched encampment or perilous pauses remain a dangerous threat to those on the way. The danger is subtle because what is intended to be a pause often turns into permanent encampment. Strewn along life's way are the souls of millions with good intentions. And the "mountains" around which we pitch "tents" are numerous. There are: dissatisfaction with leadership, feeling overlooked and ignored, moral lapses that seem insurmountable, unfaithful stewardship with time and talent, delinquent parenting, and selfishness, among others. Oh, did I forget to mention pride? Self-importance clogs the path of grace to the soul. Pride, we are told, comes before the inevitable fall.

Across millennia of humankind's broken and checkered history comes the soul-saving clarion call "You have been skirting this hill country long enough. Head north." Strike tents. Disentangle from the familiar, which, in time, seems genuine. Turn toward the promised land, for we are nearing home.

Whether by loss of perspective or paralyzing fear, many surrender to the tedium of life's challenges. Who among us have not been tempted to give up, to "encamp," to lose sight of the prize? At times, the dawn of day is preceded by the darkest night.

Indeed we are nearing home, for the land of promise lies just over the mountains. Thank God almighty, we are nearing home.

Deliverer and sustainer in this life's pilgrimage, keep us from falling victim to those experiences that tend to discourage the journey of faith. Save us from those mountains looming so large that encourage permanent encampment. Keep us focused on life's ultimate goal. Amen.

Three

B U T
The Disjunctive Conjunction
Invites Self-Inventory

Naaman, commander of the army of the king of Syria,

was a great man with his master and in high favor,

because by him, the Lord had given victory to Syria.

He was a mighty man of valor, but he was a leper.

—2 Kings 5:1 RSV

IT IS A PICTURE OF PRISTINE BEAUTY. This sharp, sleek, shining BMW sits abandoned on the shoulder of a busy highway. Its elegance is enhanced by aerodynamic lines, soft blue gray color, glistening chrome-trimmed headlights, and sporty spoke wheels with spotless whitewall tires.

A glimpse inside reveals soft leather seats, an elegantly trimmed dashboard with an ebony flair, giving a muted invitation to get behind the wheel. Sitting under the hood is a wall-to-wall engine, spotless and looking as if it has never been driven. It seems ready to enter the Daytona 500 race.

Now sit behind the steering wheel, adjust the seatbelts, position the rearview mirrors, insert the ignition key, turn it to start, and . . . hear only a click. This luxury automobile possesses every feature desired by a car enthusiast, but the engine is without power because its battery is dead.

"But," the contrasting conjunction, destroys expectations, diminishes estimates, damages reputations, disrupts well-intentioned plans, and drives to despair those without redemptive options. In relationship to the BMW, the "but" changes the positive picture of a luxury car into a dysfunctional, discarded, currently useless automobile, somewhat of a golden sorrow to its owner.

"But," when used as a contrasting conjunction in defining humans and their behavior, often diminishes or destroys positive profiles. This is the case with Naaman in the text at hand. He was captain of the host of the king of Syria. Naaman had gained honor and fame for numerous victories he had won for Syria. He was an astute military commander, and many of his campaigns were against Israel. He was a great man with his ruler. He had achieved special recognition from the crown and was honored and revered by soldiers under his command.

So here is Naaman, military commander, honored by his king, favored at the palace, revered and respected by his soldiers, feared by his enemies, mighty and valorous in battle, praised by Syrians for his numerous victories, "but" he suffered from leprosy (2 Kings 5:1). This "but," a conjunction of contrast, diminishes Naaman's positive image so clearly detailed in the text. In other words, he is not all that he seems to be; there is a flaw in his life that restricts him from social circles. In fact, he was socially ostracized.

Leprosy was severely feared, and those inflicted with the disease were deemed unclean and excluded from society. The thirteenth chapter of the book of Leviticus describes in great detail the expansive rituals developed to deal with those diagnosed with leprosy. Severe social stigma was applied to the leprous person.

"The person who has the leprous disease shall wear torn clothes and let the hair of his head be disheveled; and he shall cover his upper lip and cry out, 'Unclean, unclean.' He shall remain unclean as long as he has the disease; he is unclean. He shall live alone; his dwelling shall be outside the camp" (Lev. 13:45–46). In addition to physical discomfort and pain, the leper endures the lash of social ostracism. Naaman had all the marks of military distinction and favorable treatment by his king; he was a VIP in Syria, but the author of the book of Kings says, "But he was a leper."

He was not all that his office and prominence made him in the public eye. There was a serious flaw, one that triggered his quest for a cure from the very nation against whom he had won many battles.

Suggested by his servant maid, an Israelite whom he had taken captive in one of his military campaigns against Israel, he sought healing from Elisha, the prophet. Naaman pocketed his pride, allayed his anger, obeyed the directives of the prophet, and was healed. Complete obedience—God is particular.

The story of Naaman is informative. We are not all that we seem. There are "buts" in our lives that inhibit spiritual growth and effective witnessing. Often they seem small and inconsequential, but it is the little foxes that spoil the vine. A little jealousy unabated turns into hatred; an occasional dishonesty blossoms into a major fraud; half a truth becomes a whole lie; a little tardiness grows into practiced procrastination.

We may occupy the highest office in our church. We may be present in every church service and business meeting. We may be celebrated as a most effective preacher or command the largest following as a televangelist. We may meet all the tenets of faithful stewardship from a monetary perspective and be seen as a model disciple. It is very possible for someone to achieve distinction, favor, and honor by public acclaim, and at the end of the day hear one say, "He was such a committed and devoted Christian, even though. . . ."

The insidious danger of these seemingly insignificant "thoughs" in our lives is that they often remain unnoticed and nonthreatening. Vividly do I recall a conversation with a fellow soccer player as we walked from the soccer field back to the college campus. Passing a tree with some attractive berries, my friend picked some and began eating. Turning to him I said, "Roy, I understand that those berries are a slow poison." His retort was quick and humorous, "I am not in any hurry," he said. If it is slow, it's ok, is the implied message. Often we treat the "buts" with the same levity and unconcern with which Roy dealt with those potentially dangerous berries.

Silently, imperceptibly, but destructively these little foxes, these "buts" and flaws, nibble at our character. Left unresolved, they eventually inhibit spiritual maturity. A giant pine tree stood beside my study window defying hurricane-force winds, torrential rains, freezing cold, and sizzling summer suns for many years. One day I noticed that its needles were turning brown and thought that it was a seasonal change. I was in error; it was dying. Some small insects had entered the trunk of that giant pine and over months had imperceptibly nibbled it to death. What the unforgiving elements could not do, those little "foxes" accomplished.

This spiritual reflection exhorts self-inventory, self-examination in light of the high calling of God in our Lord Jesus Christ. This challenge is promising because we are saved by hope. Naaman sought healing through the advice of his maid, a captive from the land of his enemy. Renouncing pride and prejudice he humbly dipped seven times in the Jordan River, as instructed by Elisha. He returned to his homeland healed and a believer in the Creator of heaven and earth. His was both a physical and a spiritual healing.

"But" as a contrasting conjunction appears elsewhere in scripture where it contrasts God's saving grace to the evil, destructive devices of the devil, the prince and power of the domain of evil. Writing to the Ephesians, Paul describes life dominated by the evil one. "All of us once lived among them in the passions of our flesh . . . and we were by nature children of wrath, like everyone else. But God, who is rich in mercy . . . made us alive together with Christ—by grace you have been saved . . ." (Eph. 2:3–5).

The prince of power is about, but God; you were fulfilling the desires of the flesh, but God; your minds were slaves to evil machinations, but God; you were by nature children of wrath, but God is merciful, indeed "rich in mercy." God has given us life and hope, having saved us by grace. The conjunction of contrast that diminishes is replaced by the conjunction of contrast that saves. Glory and praise be to the Almighty who transmutes flaws into faith, and buts into beatitudes.

Does this message call for critical self-examination? Is there a debilitating flaw in your life so nocuous by its potency and dangerous by its "invisibility" that it calls for a conscious effort for fervent self-inventory?

God, thank you for exercising patience with our repentant following and faltering faith. Forgive our moments of doubts and inability to remember your faithfulness that is new every morning. Create within us the desire to examine ourselves and to seek refuge in the richness of your grace. Amen.

Four

RUNNING WITHOUT THE MESSAGE
Zeal without Knowledge

The king said, "Is it well with the young man
Absalom?" Ahimaaz answered, "When Joab sent your
servant, I saw a great tumult, but I do not know what
it was." The king said, "Turn aside, and stand here."
So he turned aside, and stood still.

—2 Samuel 18:29–30

But in your hearts sanctify Christ as Lord.
Always be ready to make your defense to anyone who
demands from you an accounting for the hope that is
in you; yet do it with gentleness and reverence.

—1 Peter 3:15–16a

THE QUEST FOR CERTAINTY is pervasive and universal among humans. It intensifies when critical decisions affecting life, values, family, and religious beliefs are involved. Credibility, reliability, replicability, and specificity are basic ingredients in satisfying this quest, for finitude needs promise and hope predicated on the best possible evidence.

I believe that at no other time in human history has the quest for certainty and truth been more global and intense. Inheriting the technology and information of the past century, the twenty-first century pursues relentlessly areas untouched by past generations. Medical science and genetics have penetrated the formula of genes, the basic unit of life that determines individual characteristics, a scientific breakthrough with ominous possibilities, including cloning.

Because the media transmitting information are so pervasive and worldwide, knowledge is being homogenized. Our television screens bring instantaneous information from around the globe, so together, we share the same information.

Instantaneity is just one critical characteristic of this information age. Wide consumption of the same information accentuates the need for reliability and replicability. Without these tests, credibility and, consequently, certainty are compromised.

Transmitting information, "running with the message," the certifiable message is ultimately more critical when decisions affecting life depend on it. Some life and death decisions are irreversible; here, certainty is necessary. Devastating are those decisions made on information given by one "running without the message."

Rebellion and insurrection helped tarnish the reign of David, king of Israel. His son, Absalom, led the insurrection to dethrone him. Marshaling some rebellious Israelites, Absalom engaged his father's army in numerous skirmishes throughout the kingdom of Israel. Joab, commander of David's forces, received the king's message that Absalom's life should be spared, despite his rebellion. David's wishes were clear. "Deal gently for my sake with the young man, even Absalom," said David.

However, in the heat of battle Absalom was caught in a tree by his copious hair and was left hanging, as the mule he rode went from under him. Against King David's wishes, he was slain and buried in the woods.

David awaited the outcome of the battle and the fate of his beloved, albeit rebellious son. Joab, his commander in chief, had the daunting task of informing the king that his son had died in battle. This devastating news had to be accurate and verifiable. It had to be borne by someone who had been in battle, who could give primary evidence. It had to be a soldier who had seen.

Choosing a Cushite, Joab dispatched him with the news and instruction to David, "Go tell the king what you have seen." While the Cushite was on his way, Ahimaaz, another servant of David's, entreated Joab to let him run to the king with the news. "You are not to carry tidings today," said Joab. "You may carry tidings another day, but today you shall not do so, because the king's son is dead." Joab continues, "Why will you run, my son, seeing that you have no reward?" In essence, Joab was saying to this servant that it is irresponsible, indeed misleading, to run without the message needed by this anxiety-ridden father.

"I will run" anyway, said this man without the message. And Joab said, "Run." Physically equipped, but lacking relevant information, Ahimaaz outran the Cushite, and when the king heard that Ahimaaz was running to him David said, "He is a good man, and comes with good tidings." But soon we will discover that goodness is necessary but not sufficient in bringing good tidings, in bringing truth.

A revealing conversation took place between the king and his "good" servant. Assuming the reverent posture before the king, Ahimaaz began telling David all that he thought the king wanted to hear. He stated how the God had destroyed the evil rebellious men who had taken up arms against Israel. But these were all generalities. The king needed a specific message. "Is it well with the young man Absalom?" he asked.

The moment of truth arrived and here was the answer: "When Joab sent your servant, I saw a great tumult, but I do not know what it was" (2 Sam. 18:29). Here was zeal without knowledge. There is no question that Ahimaaz was greatly devoted to King David. In fact, the king called him a good man (see verses 19–33). Unquestionable devotion and unquenchable zeal, however, cannot satisfy the need for critical information—for the good tidings.

The sad sequel to this meeting between the king and his zealous servant is reported in verse 30. "The king said, 'Turn aside, and stand here.' So he turned aside, and stood still." This servant had to step aside because generalities about success in the war were a message but not the message for that moment in time. As he stood aside, perhaps feeling dejected and deflated, the man with the message, whom he had outrun, arrived. Responding to the king's primary concern, "Is it well with the young man Absalom?" the Cushite responded in the negative, a response that brought great grief to the king, but it was relevant information.

Our age has crowned information as "king." The messenger, the medium, and the message must be credible, reliable, and available. This is no time to run without a message. The Apostle Peter challenges all believers. "But in your hearts sanctify Christ as Lord. Always be ready to make your defense to anyone who demands from you an accounting for the hope that is in you" (1 Pet. 3:15).

Effective witnessing requires three basic elements found in the text. A prerequisite is the primacy of Christ in the lives of believers. Peter says, "But in your hearts sanctify Christ as Lord." The word sanctify carries such connotations as sacredness, inviolability, hallowedness, unassailability, and setting apart. Each implies the special, primary place that Jesus occupies in the hearts of those who serve him. His transcendence in hearts relegates every other human endeavor to a second tier. It is this hallowed place that anticipates and mandates the second element in Peter's exhortation.

Readiness is the watchword of those in whose hearts Jesus is sanctified. This information age, dominated by precision technology, demands facts immediately. Our push-button culture wants it all and wants it now. No information is as important as the good news on which human destiny rests. Readiness requires daily repentant following. Readiness is a consequence of prayerful perusal of the Word. The Apostle Paul admonishes, "Do your best to present yourself to God as one approved by God, a worker who has no need to be ashamed, rightly explaining the word of truth" (2 Tim. 2:15). Knowledge of the Word is not restricted to preachers; it includes all those in whose hearts Jesus is Lord.

Sanctification precedes readiness and readiness demands specificity. Peter says be ready to give a reason for the hope. Why is Jesus Lord? How was that conclusion reached? What noticeable effect has this experience had on lives of those declaring this hope? This information age is calling not only for instantaneous information, it seeks specificity, it seeks documentation, it demands credibility.

And credibility is enhanced by primary, firsthand information. Running with the message calls for personal, existential knowledge. Ahimaaz, king David's faithful servant, ran with great zeal, but he had no message because he had not seen the facts. So he had to stand aside. The Apostle Paul warns against zeal without knowledge. "I can testify that they have a zeal for God, but it is not enlightened" (Rom. 10:2).

Distortion of truth, roadblocks to effective proclamation of the gospel, may easily follow zealous converts who cannot give a credible reason for the hope in them. Paul exhorts that this ignorance of God's righteousness creates self-righteousness, thus enervating a basic tenet of the story of redemption, righteousness by faith.

At times the zealous person without the message creates excitement in others who experience intense disappointment when the messenger fails to deliver. A preacher friend of mine on his way to a church service got lost in a city. Driving into a fast-food parking lot, he asked a young man for directions to the church, but the young man did not know. The preacher drove back on the street into heavy traffic and waited for the traffic light to change. Suddenly he noticed the same young man running towards him gesturing to him to wait. Arriving in great haste and speaking with a stammering tone, he said, "Sir, I just asked my brother and he didn't know either."

This young man, willing to help and with noticeable enthusiasm, ran without the message to a preacher lost on his way to a church service. That preacher's disappointment was compounded by some anxiety as he held up traffic waiting for a zealous person without knowledge.

A very broken and troubled world awaits the reason for the hope within us. Credibility, readiness, and specificity are hallmarks for effectively trumpeting the gospel of peace and hope. Goodness and zeal are necessary but not sufficient elements in a posture of readiness. Knowledge, primary experience, being there, standing around the cross existentially and cognitively, all help us give the trumpet a certain sound. Then souls will cry out, "What must I do to have eternal life?"

Does the quest for meaning in your life cry out for certainty? Shouldn't your search seek that infallible source, the word of God?

God, take full possession of our hearts and develop within us the thirst and the ability to learn thy unchangeable truths in these changing times. And make us instruments in building your realm on earth, in your precious name. Amen.

Five

THE CALL FOR RELIGIOUS INTEGRITY
Walking the Talk

Ephraim mixes himself with the peoples;

Ephraim is a cake not turned.

Ephraim has become like a dove, silly and without sense;

they call upon Egypt. . . .

—Hosea 7:8, 11

THREE HUNDRED PEOPLE ATTENDED a greatly anticipated meeting in a top-rated hotel in a major capital city. Elegantly dressed couples, who had planned for months for this affair, sat down to dinner. Expectations were in keeping with costs; occasion and efforts were similarly high with regards to the cuisine. Disappointments were intense and unanimous when dinner was found insipid and unpalatable. Items were uncooked, unseasoned, and in some respects, not edible. The ambiance of that much-anticipated evening was severely damaged, for dinner was insipid.

The prophet Hosea describes the condition of Ephraim/Israel as an unbaked cake, a metaphor defining a nation as insipid, undesirable, and unfit to represent the name of Jehovah. The cake referenced in this text was a circular thin layer of bread that was quickly baked and easily burned if not flipped over and given close attention. Hosea hereby gives a graphic description of spiritual inconsistency and lack of genuine devotion to God.

Using the metaphor "cake not turned," Hosea scores the utter seriousness of Ephraim's apostasy. Ephraim, used in this context, represents the entire state of Israel, for it was the principal tribe of the northern kingdom. Why name a "cake" over other items necessary for human existence? A cake, like a meal, is absolutely required for physical health and well-being. Unbaked, uncooked—thus insipid, unpalatable, and unfit for consumption—it will be rejected, discarded, and thrown among garbage destined for destruction.

What turned Ephraim, this "cake" so initially desirable, into the nation facing rejection by God? Hosea, whose prophetic ministry lasted from 753 to 729 B.C.E., lived in the northern kingdom, Israel, at a time of national apostasy. His ministry covered the days of kings Uzziah, Hezekiah, and Jeroboam, kings who led Israel and Judah to the darkest days of national disobedience to God's commandments. Commercialism, materialism, and social evils permeated the national agenda. And as wealth increased, so did profligacy, bloodshed, injustice, and progressive denial of God's governance in the lives of rulers and people.

Called to denounce their behavior, which would yield destruction of the nation, short of national repentance, Hosea devoted his entire ministry, all fourteen chapters of the Book, to alert Ephraim about God's displeasure regarding the sinful and idolatrous behavior of the nation. Using stinging metaphors to describe the depth of spiritual decline and depravity, Hosea was unsparing in language and passion as he denounced Ephraim's disobedience and dalliance with idolatry. Perhaps proclamation of the Word in modern times is so clothed with muted messages and refined phrases that the trumpet of truth has lost that certain sound necessary to evoke the plea, "Brothers and sisters, what shall we do to inherit eternal life?"

Clarity, precision, focused brevity characterize prophetic messages in times past. "Ahab said to him [Elijah], 'Is it you, you troubler of Israel?' And he answered, 'I have not troubled Israel; but you have, and your father's house . . .'" (1 Kings 18:17–18). "Nathan said to David, 'You are the man!'" Nathan was saying to David that he was the adulterer with Bathsheba (2 Sam. 12:7). "For they have gone up to Assyria, a wild ass wandering alone. Ephraim has bargained for lovers" (Hos. 8:9).

Life and death issues demand forthrightness and uncompromising clarity. Someone aware of the tentativeness with which truth is proclaimed today asked, "Whatever happened to sin?" This question is germane given the "respectable" names by which sin is called in modern America. It is "errant behavior," "unintended mistake," "juvenile impropriety," "temporary insanity," or just "social deviance." Separated from its derivative that involves disobedience to the command of God, sin becomes a benign, perhaps socially acceptable behavior without any ultimate consequences.

Hosea was forthright, direct, clear, and uncompromising. Some may say even offensive. His litany of national sins included ignorance of God's demands, idol worship, whoredom, amalgamation with idol worshipers, poor judgment, indecisiveness, seeking assistance from Israel's enemies—Assyria and Egypt—lack of consistence in devotion to God, injustice towards the poor, priests behaving like people, political leadership (kings) engaging in disobedience, and debauchery.

This was a national apostasy—kings, priests, and people professing to be God's people but worshiping idols and adopting the ways and culture of people who knew not Jehovah. This was gross insincerity, religious hypocrisy; Ephraimites may be more precisely called religious hybrids.

Appropriately described, Ephraim is a "cake not turned," baked only on one side, partially committed to its history as God's people, by practicing idolatry. Religious schizophrenics, they were fit to be spewed out, relegated to the dustbins of history. But God, hesitant to abandon the chosen people, though they were rebellious and disobedient, sought their repentance and allegiance. Perchance they would amend their ways and return to true worship (see Hos. 11:9).

Unrepentant and rebellious, Israel was taken captive by the Assyrians and experienced deplorable treatment in captivity. Hosea bore God's last message of warning and hope to Ephraim/Israel.

Half-baked Christians: religious hybrids! Might there be some relevance in these descriptive phrases for the church of the twenty-first century? The call here is for genuine religious experience. To use a common phrase that invites consistency and credibility, the Christian church is expected to "walk the talk."

The church as a voluntary institution tends to mirror the times in which it exists. I am reminded of H. Richard Niebuhr's book *The Social Sources of Denominationalism*,[4] which provides a brilliant analysis of how social forces influence belief systems and denominational structures across the years. His volume *The Kingdom of God in America*[5] was written to correct any notion of social reductionism in the previous volume that could leave the impression that the church is a total captive of social forces. However, there is an inevitable interplay between believers' theological (vertical) commitment, and the social forces (horizontal) that provide the pragmatic context of daily living.

A church surrounded by great wealth tends to display habits and practices of the wealthy. History testifies to the abiding faith and devotion among believers in times of persecution and paucity. Where there are injustice and prejudice institutionalized by political and economic institutions, the church is either quiescent regarding it or joins oppressive forces in "baptizing" such practices by creating biblical support. The dark period of slavery in America is exhibit one.

Numerous forces in modern times impact the church. America is enjoying unprecedented wealth and prosperity. Permissiveness—whether in sex, drugs, disrespect for authority, or popular endorsement of deviant behavior—is rampant. Economic injustice is embedded in the capitalistic system. Most of America's wealth is concentrated in a few hands. The rich get richer and the poor get poorer, and the disparity widens relentlessly.

Similar temptations confront the church today as in the days of the prophet Hosea. Imperceptibly but incessantly secular forces creep into our lives and influence behavior that becomes acceptable by popular endorsement, and less culpable by routine practice. The threat here is that of split devotion, a religious schizophrenia, a kind of religious hybrid devoid of uncompromising commitment to God. This spiritual fence-straddling yields half-baked Christians, insipid, unpalatable, and unfit for the kingdom.

The Apocalypse, like Hosea, sounds a prophetic call, one addressing indecision, inconsistency, and spiritual neutrality. In warning the church at Laodicea, last of the seven churches, the prophet John prophesied, "I know your works; you are neither cold nor hot. I wish that you were either cold or hot. So because you are lukewarm, and neither cold nor hot, I am about to spit you out of my mouth" (Rev. 3:15–16).

The Laodicean church, seen as the Christian church existing at the end of probationary times, is described as indecisive and uncommitted. Its being "lukewarm" means it is sitting on the fence, without conviction, without distinction, neutral, without a vision, without a message, indeed useless to God's cause.

I believe that we are living in Laodicean times and belong to the church of these times. It is the contemporary version of the church to which the prophet Hosea preached. Ephraim was half-baked. Laodicea is lukewarm. Each is in a state unacceptable to God, ineffective stewards in God's vineyard. Prosperity was widespread in Hosea's day. Laodicea says, "I am rich, I have prospered, and I need nothing" (Rev. 3:17). Wealth, prosperity neutralizes spiritual zeal and leaves believers half-baked or lukewarm. Boasting of being rich and in need of nothing is deceptive, because the true state of members of this church is that they are "wretched, pitiable, poor, blind, and naked" (Rev. 3:17).

But there is hope. "Therefore I counsel you to buy from me gold refined by fire so that you may be rich" (Rev. 3:18a). This is an invitation to commitment, to a final decision for righteousness. Half-baked Christians can be made whole; lukewarmness can become brilliant with a zeal fired and fueled by the Holy Spirit.

Have you been tainted by the state of indecisiveness? Shouldn't all travel the road of full commitment to a noble cause?

Father, be patient with us and send the Holy Spirit to convict and inspire us to be faithful followers. Thank you for abundant grace that is greater than all our sins. Amen.

Six

SINKING IN FAMILIAR WATERS
Life in a Rut

He said, "Come." So Peter got out of the boat,
started walking on the water, and came toward Jesus.
But when he noticed the strong wind, he became
frightened, and beginning to sink,
he cried out, "Lord, save me!"

—Matthew 14:29, 30

LIFE'S FORMIDABLE CHALLENGES CONFRONT US when the familiar meets the unknown; when novelty invades the routine; when ingrained habits and calcified ideas encounter new patterns of thinking, new behavioral expectations. A life patterned by the passage of procedure, thus tied inextricably to the past, is life in a rut.

The fallacy of the familiar may create a false certainty. I heard someone say that we should not make the same mistake twice, that it is better to make two different mistakes if the effort is to break out of the past. The popular saying, "familiarity breeds contempt," carries some currency; it is critically germane to our subject if contempt is resistance to explore new ideas, to engage in objective self-examination, to prepare for an unexpected turn or potential tragedy along life's way.

The unexamined life, which someone says is not worth living, may leave us sinking in familiar waters. Our text says that "when he [Peter] noticed the strong wind, he became frightened, and beginning to sink, he cried out, 'Lord save me!'"

This fourteenth chapter of Matthew describes an incident most insightful and informative for the faithful follower who seems to be doing everything according to the book but, challenged by adversity or some potentially tragic circumstance, loses faith and initiates a journey of spiritual retrogression. In Peter's case, he was sinking in familiar waters.

Jesus had just fed the five thousand souls. Tired from a long day of ministering, he sought a quiet place in the mountain to pray and rest. After sending his disciples to take a ship across the Sea of Galilee to the land of Gerasenes, he retired to the mountain. A boisterous, life-threatening wind created a storm that tossed the ship and the disciples about in its angry waves.

But someone was watching that ship and its valuable passengers. They would be bearers of the good tidings to the ends of the then known world. And Jesus would not allow the forces of hell to destroy them. That someone watching was Jesus. At about four or five in the morning, he came walking on the water. Peter recognized him and asked to join the Lord by walking on the waves. Stepping out on the waves at the Lord's invitation, Peter did well for a while but lost faith as winds lashed around him, and he began to sink. Sinking, Peter cried for help, "Lord, save me." The ruler of earth, sea, and sky stretched out his hands and lifted his disciple from certain death.

Why did you doubt, asked Jesus? For the faithful follower, many are the lessons taught by this early morning divine/human drama on the Sea of Galilee. In the first place, responding to the call to serve does not promise a life without adversity. The shipload of disciples was on a mission sent and sanctioned by Jesus. At times, that very mission angers the forces of evil, and obstacles appear in the path of the servants of God that defy explanation. Could the storm that night be one of those obstacles?

In the second place, even the sincerity of the faithful is not without times of doubt. I think no one would question the sincerity and commitment of the disciples who, the prior evening, saw an amazing display of compassion and power when Jesus fed five thousand people. Now in the trial of faith, doubt surfaced, and Peter started to sink. Earlier in this volume, I described the path of discipleship as "repentant following" since faith is not totally without times of doubt. Jesus did not condemn Peter and his colleagues because there were lapses of faith. He simply asked and demonstrated that there was room for growth.

Another lesson, a daunting one, is that Peter was "sinking in familiar waters." The Sea of Galilee was familiar territory to Peter. As a boy, he must have swum in it and played on its beaches. He was a fisherman when Jesus called him and Andrew, his brother. In fact, they were by the sea when Jesus invited them to follow him and become fishers of men. He saw that sea when it was calm; he had endured the strong waves of storms past; he knew the landmarks to guide him back to shore. These were familiar waters, and Peter, who had spent his life in and around the Sea of Galilee, was sinking in its angry waves.

The subtlety of the familiar lies in its routine rituals and practices, which dull the desire for change. It establishes a comfort zone, an untouchable sanctuary, sometimes a know-all posture impenetrable, at times, even by truth. In worship, all must kneel to pray or it is not worshipful; only the King James Version of the Bible is inspired, no other version bears truth; eleven on Sabbath mornings is the only appropriate hour for regular worship service. And the list goes on ad infinitum.

Such veneration of the past stifles spiritual and intellectual growth. The future is to be guided by the past, not to be impeded by it. And the future should not ignore the wisdom of the past, for we know where we are going because of where we have been. The church must develop the posture and skill to deal with the dynamics of continuity and change.

Longevity of church membership is not the final barometer of spiritual maturity. Longstanding pastorates are not necessarily the most nurturing and productive. Doctrinal affirmation need not be the final word on truth. The true test of discipleship resides in the prayer of that man in the scriptures, "Lord, I believe; help thou my unbelief."

Sinking in familiar waters, calcified concepts, bottling of old wines, refusal to grow beyond the infantile status of the new convert means progressive spiritual retrogression and ultimate spiritual death. Paul writes against spiritual stagnation: "For though by this time you ought to be teachers, you need someone to teach you again the basic elements of the oracles of God. You need milk, not solid food" (Heb. 5:12). Paul continues his critique of intellectual laziness: "But solid food is for the mature, for those whose faculties have been trained by practice to distinguish good from evil" (Heb. 5:14). Following verses of this chapter promote intellectual and spiritual growth, for they equip the faithful with the capacity to discern between good and evil.

Jesus uses an agricultural metaphor to punctuate the need and pattern of the growth of God's dominion: "The earth produces of itself, first the stalk, then the head, then the full grain in the head" (Mark 4:28). Progression, growth, development, change—these define the path of the faithful. Any other paradigm possesses the threat of sinking in familiar waters.

Thanks be to God, there is hope for the sinking soul. There is hope when the believer is brought to realize a need for renewal, the state of spiritual stagnation, the danger of comfort only with the familiar. The realization may not be as dramatic as Peter's physical descent into the raging sea, but the metaphor is clear. Even as he was sinking physically because of doubt, souls are sinking spiritually as they remain "immature" in the Word.

Does your life seem to be going nowhere? Are you afraid of the unknown, the unfamiliar? Do you settle for nonproductive self-complacency? As you struggle to reach beyond the waves of doubt and are challenged by seeming insurmountable obstacles, are you tempted to give up? Don't, for there is hope.

Peter cried, "Lord, save me!" Jesus was there, and on time. As he lifted Peter from the engulfing waves, he stands ready to lift every desiring soul who is gradually sinking in the sea of satisfaction with the status quo, the familiar, with spiritual stagnation. A personal testimony in the song "Love Lifted Me" speaks of the efficacy of God's saving grace:

> *I was sinking deep in sin, far from the peaceful shore,*
> *Very deeply stained within, sinking to rise no more;*
> *But the Ruler of the sea heard my despairing cry,*
> *From the waters lifted me, now safe am I.*

> *All my heart to Him I give, ever to Him I'll cling,*
> *In his blessed presence live, ever His praises sing.*
> *Love so mighty and so true merits my soul's best songs;*
> *Faithful, loving service to Him belongs.*

Souls in danger, look above, Jesus completely saves;
He will lift you by His love out of the angry waves.
He's the Master of the sea, billows His will obey;
He your Savior wants to be saved today.

CHORUS: *Love lifted me, Love lifted me,*
When nothing else could help, Love lifted me.[6]

PART TWO

Life's Unfinished Task:
Called to Service

Seven

WHAT ARE YOU DOING HERE?

When Elijah heard it, he wrapped his face
in his mantle and went out and stood at the entrance
of the cave. Then there came a voice to him that said,
"What are you doing here, Elijah?"

—1 Kings 19:13

GOD'S CALL TO SERVICE reaches the candidate at the most unexpected places. That call may come at one's work place; Gideon received his while threshing wheat by the "winepress." Elisha was plowing his field when he was enlisted for prophetic service, Amos was a herdsman, Peter was fishing, Paul was persecuting, and John Wesley felt his heart "strangely warmed" in a religious service. Legitimacy of the call to service rests not on where or when but on whom God deems fittest for a particular ministry. Repeatedly, the call comes to busy people, those engaged, the industrious.

The second call for prophetic service came to Elijah as he hid in a cave. It was initiated with a question, "What are you doing here, Elijah?" It is a question with most profound implications. It certainly was asking how someone of his caliber and experience could have fallen from peaks of victories in the cause of service to the valley of despond, in flight from a heathen worshipper, hiding in a cave.

The question implies that Elijah had lost a sense of history. The facts of history are critical for maintaining an unshakable faith. Repeatedly, prophets called to chastise Israel for their disobedience to God's commandments recited the history of their miraculous delivery from Egyptian slavery, provisions for their physical needs, protection from hostile nations, and settlement in the land of promise.

In parabolic mode, the prophet Isaiah describes Israel's special place in God's plan, and God's tender treatment towards this chosen nation: "Let me sing for my beloved my love-song concerning his vineyard; My beloved had a vineyard on a very fertile hill. He dug it and cleared it of stones, and planted it with choice vines; he built a watchtower in the midst of it, and hewed out a wine vat in it; he expected it to yield grapes, but it yielded wild grapes" (Isa. 5:1–2). Appeal to history raises the question of fidelity, ungratefulness, and just common sense.

So, Elijah, given all that I have accomplished through your ministry in the recent past, what are you doing here? Although King Ahab has done more than all previous kings to provoke me, and has destroyed the holy altars in Israel and established the worship of Baal, you dramatically reminded him of his transgression and the need to repair the broken-down altars and reestablish the worship of the Maker of heaven and earth. You informed Ahab, that because of his evil behavior, a long drought would afflict Israel, and during the drought I sustained you by the brook Cherith.

The rainless season was long, the brook dried up, and I sent to you the widow of Zarephath, who took care of you. When I had adequately received Ahab's attention, you were instructed to announce to Ahab that the drought would cease and rain would fall, and the rains came.

The crowning act of your ministry was the critical and historic meeting between you and the prophets of Baal on Mount Carmel. There you had nine hundred false prophets of Baal slain and proved beyond any reasonable doubt that Jehovah is the Lord of heaven and earth. All Israelites present on Carmel, after seeing the miraculous display of God's power cried, "The Lord, he is the God; the Lord, he is the God."

And now, threatened by Jezebel, Ahab's idol-worshipping wife, you have fled to Horeb, a journey of forty days and forty nights, a journey so long that I had to feed you along the way. And after all those mighty acts of God done through and for you, here you are hiding out in a cave on mount Horeb. "What are you doing here Elijah?"

Pertinent lessons for the faithful follower reside in this text:

- Fear inevitably replaces faith when the facts of history are forgotten. Hope in human experience rests on God's unchangeable character; God is the same yesterday, today, and forever. Someone has written that we have no fear for the future, except as we forget the way God has led us. Learn to stand on the promises of God.

- Success is not an antidote to self-pity. Elijah experienced a large dose of self-pity when in response to the question regarding his flight to a cave, he declared his fidelity to God, indeed his jealousy for "the Lord God of hosts" when every one else in Israel, including the prophets, had either forsaken the Lord of Hosts or was slain. "I alone am left, and they are seeking my life, to take it away" (1 Kings 19:9–10).

  In fact, Elijah's self-pity was unfounded based on the facts. There were seven thousand Israelites who had not converted to Baal worship. They remained faithful to the true God. Even this prominent prophet who could predict drought and pray successfully for rain, defy and eliminate hundreds of false prophets, pray for miraculous consuming of sacrifice, and bring back to life the dead son of the widow of Zarephath, even he did not recall the facts regarding the people he was representing. Self-pity, an inhibiting attitude, destroys self-worth and dulls the desire for ministry.

- Subliminally or by way of a conscious, calculated decision, Elijah fled to a propitious place; he fled to Horeb, the mount of God (1 Kings 19:8; Ex. 24:13). Horeb and Sinai represent the same mountain chain in scripture. Moses ascended this mountain twice to receive the tablets of commandments from God, whose presence overshadowed the mount. If Elijah sought regeneration for a flickering faith, he chose the appropriate venue. He went to the mount of God. If you are to fall, fall facing Calvary's cross.

  Anticipating some action from God, Elijah was able to discern a revelatory event so critical to his rehabilitation and future ministry. He recognized that God was not in the boisterous rock-breaking wind or in the earthquake or fire. These spectacular displays of divine power do not necessarily reach the soul. They may evoke fear, but not faith. Not in the wind, earthquake, or fire was God found, but in a "still small voice." A voice of invitation. It is a voice that reaches the souls of men and women still shackled by the load of sin. It is a voice that says, "Come to me, all you that are weary and are carrying heavy burdens, and I will give you rest." Although the Almighty may choose to display the divine presence in fear-generating natural phenomena, God chose to speak to Elijah in a voice that calmed the fearful soul of the prophet.

■ Elijah's prophetic mission was incomplete. God had three activities that only he was commissioned to perform. What are you doing here, Elijah, when your ministry calls for immediate action? Go down to Damascus and crown Hazael king over Syria; get over into Israel and crown Jehu, the son of Nimshi, king over Israel. And now that your earthly ministry is about to come to an end, search for a man named Elisha. You will find him plowing in a field; pass him your mantle, for he will be your successor.

These were most significant assignments for a man hiding out in a cave on Mount Horeb. Indeed it is the mount of God; it may provide a refreshing pause for regeneration, but not for a flight in resignation. For at the point of self-pity, fear, and resignation, the most effective service in God's cause may be waiting. Anointing Elisha to succeed him was Elijah's crowning act as a prophet. Elisha's ministry proved even more extensive than his predecessor's.

What are you doing here and now in your following, fellow believer? Is there some frightening threat that has spawned a paralyzing fear? Has success in your ministry that has not generated expected praise propelled you into a state of apathetic self-pity? Have you withdrawn into a "cave" of inactivity while God's urgent missions go unattended?

If you are still on the "mount of God," still waiting to hear that still small voice of assurance, the Holy Spirit says "Go tell it on the mountains and everywhere that there is a need to hear the good news." This is a call for self-examination regardless of the Christian vocation or status we occupy. Elijah was given a second chance; he embraced it and finished his ministry in a chariot of fire, a blazingly benedictory gesture from heaven. Let's answer the blessed call for service.

Dear God of the wind, earthquake, and fire, speak to waiting, erring souls with that still, small voice of assurance. Draw us out of our caves of self-pity, fear, and resignation, and send us out into the vineyard. Amen.

Eight

A SECOND CHANCE SALVAGES A JOURNEY OF DISOBEDIENCE

> *Now the word of the Lord came to Jonah*
> *son of Amittai, saying "Go at once to Nineveh, that great*
> *city, and cry out against it; for their wickedness has come*
> *up before me." But Jonah set out to flee to Tarshish from*
> *the presence of the Lord. He went down to Joppa and*
> *found a ship going to Tarshish; so he paid his fare*
> *and went on board, to go with them to Tarshish,*
> *away from the presence of the Lord.*

—Jonah 1:1–3

> *The word of the Lord came to Jonah a second time,*
> *saying, "Get up, go to Nineveh, that great city, and*
> *proclaim to it the message that I tell you." So Jonah set*
> *out and went to Nineveh, according to the word of the*
> *Lord. Now Nineveh was an exceedingly large city,*
> *a three days' walk across."*

—Jonah 3:1–3

WOULD THE CERTAINTY of God's call deter us from making a detour from his appointed destination? In our finite perspectives, are we tempted by fear or fortune to choose another way? In observing fellow travelers, especially those revered, do their detours, as we perceive them, tend to impact our own call and determination to be obedient to the divine mission?

As a freshman seminarian at a college in Jamaica, West Indies, I was ablaze with energy and enthusiasm regarding the prospect and promise of pastoral service. Upper classmen exuded contagious charisma that helped solidify my commitment to the ministerial call.

One senior was especially impressive and offered the greatest promise in successful ministry. He possessed an overpowering presence. Tall, handsome, well-spoken, bright, studious, eloquent, and focused, he seemed to have it all. Expectations were unanimous; if any student were going to be eminently successful in the ministry, he would be the one.

He finished that seminary with high marks and came to the United States for further studies in ministry. We waited to hear of his brilliant seminarian exploits in America and subsequent outstanding pastoral leadership. But we waited in vain. This most promising young man made a detour. In a large American city he was seen disheveled and unkempt, walking the streets, bereft of focus and mission, a far cry from the promising prospect of a model minister he envisioned and we expected when he walked the hallowed ground of that Jamaican seminary.

Often have I reflected on the experience of that young man and the impact he has had on my own journey. He started (was sent) on an honorable road of service, but he took a "ship to Tarshish," where Tarshish means deviation from the divine call, a detour from God's highway. In the end, such detours prove disastrous, disappointing, and defeating.

Jonah, the prophet, lived in northern Palestine, northeast of Samaria. God called him to go on a mission of mercy, indeed a challenging one. He was sent to Nineveh, the capital city of Assyria, to cry out against its "wickedness" that was most gross in God's sight. This was not the most exciting or promising evangelistic mission for a "minor" prophet, one evidently inexperienced and fearful.

Frightened and apprehensive, Jonah initiated a flight. He went down to the seaport of Joppa and purchased a ticket to Tarshish, a place south of Spain and close to Gibraltor. Tarshish was twenty-two hundred miles away from Joppa, but no distance from God's presence. Jonah must have been a poor theologian unaware of God's omnipresence. The journey to Tarshish was life threatening. Lives and cargo were almost destroyed when a "great wind" sent by God attacked the boat. Jonah was identified as the cause of their dilemma and the solution was to throw him overboard.

Miraculously, God preserved Jonah and got him to land, for God's plan must not be aborted. From the bowels of the ocean, God brought Jonah to the shore and displayed forgiveness as these verses record. "The word of the Lord came to Jonah a second time, saying, 'Get up, go to Nineveh, that great city, and proclaim to it the message that I tell you'" (Jon. 3:1, 2).

God gives a second chance even to those who have shunned God's commanded mission and have taken "ships to Tarshish." Indeed, salvation by grace is a second-chance experience in the redemptive process. Contained in the Jonah episode are the seeds of God's redemptive plan that received full-blown treatment in the New Testament. The errant soul through grace receives another chance to repent and recommit to the ways of righteousness. In so doing, the soul receives a new birth and reenters the mission of building God's dominion on earth. Leaving the "ship to Tarshish," the journey of disobedience and flight from God's appointed mission, the regenerated soul takes the message of hope to the "Ninevites" who know not the God that gives a second chance through grace.

Embracing his second chance, Jonah entered the city of Nineveh and warned the people of impending doom. Building himself a booth at the east end of Nineveh, he waited to see its destruction. But Jonah must have been the most successful evangelist in recorded history. The entire city, king, people, and beasts, engaged in rituals of repentance and confession. By covering themselves in sackcloth and ashes, ancient rituals of mourning and penitence, they sought God's forgiveness. So repentant was the king that he commanded a citywide response to Jonah's message. An evil city heeded the call to repentance (see chapter 3).

God uses effectively those who disembark the "ships to Tarshish," and faithfully prosecute the mission of spreading the good tidings. Dimensions of Evangelist Jonah's effective ministry in that Assyrian city are most impressive and informative. In the first place, a reborn, regenerated soul responding to God's call may convert a city. Redemption is not restricted to any socioeconomic class; it may run the gamut from the throne to the tribe's most humble member.

Jonah 1:2 says, "Go at once to Nineveh, that great city; and cry out against it; for their wickedness has come up before me."

Certainly this was a daunting challenge for the fearful Jonah; he was sent to the capital of Assyria, a powerful nation in history, sent to a "great city," one of "three days' journey," to engage in an urban campaign. And as every evangelist knows, the sophisticated urbanites with myriad distractions tend to be less attentive and responsive to religious matters. This is true in spite of the multiple church steeples piercing the sky in our nation's cities. Of the millions swarming our cities, a relatively small number is significantly involved in church life. Another possible legitimate concern of this inexperienced evangelist is his nationality as a Palestinian taking a monotheistic religion to Assyrians not known to be worshipers of Jehovah.

Jonah fully expected destruction of Nineveh. In his booth, sitting east of the city, he waited patiently for its obliteration. But God forgave and saved the city because its inhabitants repented and changed their evil ways. Such spectacular feat in converting a city of six thousand souls to the ways of righteousness, as Jonah's campaign accomplished, would project any modern evangelist, with all the props provided by modern technology, into a preaching phenomenon.

But Jonah was exceedingly angry at his success (Jon. 4:1). His expectations of the Nineveh campaign were very different from God's. He was angry for at least three reasons:

- He anticipated that God would extend mercy to Nineveh and save the city. That is the reason he gave to board that ship to Tarshish. "That is why I fled to Tarshish at the beginning; for I knew that you are a gracious God and merciful, slow to anger, and abounding in steadfast love, and ready to relent from punishing" (verse 2). Here was a messenger, unschooled in God's redemptive plan, but instrumental in converting a city.

- The second reason for this preacher's anger was his disdain for the Assyrians. Intense enmity existed between these two nations. Jonah could not conceive of redemption being extended to Assyrians. The Gospel was yet to be announced to the world so prophetic expectations were limited and regional. So Jonah misread his mission to Nineveh.

■ In the third place, Jonah's anger was personal. His ego came into play, an ego so wounded that he preferred death than face the "disgrace" attendant to a false prophet. "Forty days more, and Nineveh shall be overthrown!" he announced (Jon. 3:4). He fully expected destruction rather than redemption. It was beyond his comprehension that if destruction of the city was the only option, announcing it was superfluous, and unnecessary. Why announce doom if it is inevitable? He misread God's plan for Nineveh.

Despite these limitations in Jonah, God used him to save a city and establish God's name in Assyria. Was Jonah misled in his prophetic announcement that in forty days Nineveh would be overthrown? No, because prophecy, as it relates to human behavior, is often governed by conditionality. If divine inflexibility governed God's dealings with humanity, promises of redemption would be irrelevant. The marks of original sin reinforced by the contradictions inherent in our nature (see the Introduction to this volume), cause the faithful to agonize like Paul, "For I do not do the good I want, but the evil I do not want is what I do" (Rom. 7:19).

The conditionality of prophetic utterances is supported by numerous passages from the Scriptures. Deuteronomy 11:13–14 states, "If you will only heed his every commandment that I am commanding you today—loving the Lord your God, and serving him with all your heart and with all your soul—then he will give the rain for your land in its season, the early rain and the later rain, and you will gather in your grain, your wine, and your oil." Clearly human responses influence certain divine acts in history, a fact Jonah failed to apply to his ministry in Nineveh.

The metaphor, "ships to Tarshish," summons each follower to self-examination. Each believer is assigned a Christian vocation, a calling appropriate to one's station in life. Whether we serve as a professional, a hired hand in manual labor, or a retiree enjoying the fruits of prior service, a faithful follower is always in God's service. Each is a builder of God's realm, an assignment that is lifelong and continual. To supercede this calling with other mundane, though necessary, activity is to embark on a ship to Tarshish.

Does your call for service bring paralyzing fear? Does the magnitude of the mission seem insurmountable? If so, recall the vacillating Jonah who converted a city.

There is hope for the soul who is on that journey. The word of God now comes the second time, "Get up and go." May the response be, "Here am I, send me."

Eternal God, without a second chance, earth's inhabitants would have no hope, for all have fallen from the state of innocence. As faltering followers, we seek empowerment to avoid taking "ships to Tarshish" thus pursuing your blueprint for our lives. May the ministry of Jonah be a consistent reminder that our life's mission must be in accordance to your will. Amen.

Nine

A BLUEPRINT FOR MODERN YOUTH

There is a boy here who has
five barley loaves and two fish. But what are
they among so many people?

—John 6:9

PARENTS HAVE NUMEROUS CHALLENGES. Providing for the physical and cultural needs of children is a formidable, unending task, especially in the younger years. But there is no more important God-given parental assignment than inculcating spiritual, traditional values in offspring. The home should be the spiritual and cultural incubator of a community, a nation, a world. As goes the home, so goes our world. Scripture, by implication, reinforces the profound responsibility of parents. Proverbs 22:6 instructs, "Train children in the right way, and when old, they will not stray."

Methods of training differ greatly. They run the gamut from strict adherence to stipulated expectations and rules to the Dr. Spock method of freedom where control is limited, discipline is rare or not stringent, and the child is allowed to follow proclivities and inclinations, the interruption of which purportedly inhibits growth and creativity. If the current generation of youth, which seems to disdain all forms of authority, legal, parental, academic and ecclesiastical, is the direct consequence of Spock's paradigm, then a libertarian approach to training children is not only suspect, but disastrous.

Parents who adhere to the biblical method of "training," a method that demands compliance with stipulated procedures and expectations, encounter forces in society that profoundly impede their efforts. Young people feed daily on a fare served by mass media that is infused with violence, pornography, explicit sex, disrespect for authority, spousal abuse, and, often, no focus on the religious factor.

Compounding the effort to train our youth are the boon and bane of what is called the "information age." Indeed, technology has profoundly influenced the method, accessibility, and speed with which information is received and disseminated today. The computer has made time and space irrelevant. It brings information here and takes us there with uncanny swiftness. These times may be called the age of immediacy—immediate information, immediate gratification, immediate responses, and immediate solutions.

But the information age is also a bane; some even call it a curse. With the same alacrity, it brings into homes very undesirable information pictorially and audiovisually. In an uncontrolled environment, youngsters feed on questionable, at times corrupting information, which places them one step away from behaving in consonance with what they see and hear.

So the challenge of parenting and training children in the way they should go places a critical but daunting responsibility on parents. If some measure of sanity and traditional values is to be reintroduced into our communities and nation, the point of departure must be our homes.

As we seek a model for young people, a blueprint to guide in parental efforts, the Gospel of John presents a boy whom Andrew introduces as "There is a boy here" (John 6:9). Beginning with the first verse of chapter 6, the Apostle John describes a scene of human hunger, both spiritual and physical, divine compassion, altruism, and miraculous intervention. Intending to feed the multitude, Jesus asked Phillip, "Where are we to buy bread for these people to eat?" Phillip's response, "Six months' wages would not buy enough bread for each of them to get a little," is an affirmation of both realism and mistaken identity—realism because this was a first in his experience. Feeding five thousand hungry men in addition to women and children does seem impossible, especially absent available resources.

Phillip's realism really resides in mistaken identity. He identified the ruler with the ordinary, the limited, and the powerless. It had not yet sunk into his mind that the Questioner was the Ruler of earth, sea, and sky. Further, he missed the significance in the "we" in Jesus' question. "Where are we to buy bread," asks Jesus. Here is divinity linking with humanity for ministry. Absence of this linkage brings not only legitimate doubt but inexorable failure. So many efforts to serve, so many campaigns fired by human compassion, so many lofty ideals established but unrealized, so many giants have fallen in the agelong struggle between the forces of good and evil because the "we" formula has been underutilized.

But we must get to the text, "There is a boy here." Where Phillip failed, Andrew, Simon Peter's brother, found someone with five barley loaves and two fishes, and disclosing the news to Jesus said, "There is a boy here," among the thousands, among adults, women with children, pilgrims preparing for the upcoming Passover. Among fishermen from the sea of Tiberias was this boy attending an open-air service, listening to the Ruler preacher. This boy possessed sterling characteristics that make him a model, a blueprint for our youth of today.

He chose to meet Jesus. Hearing marvelous things about this man Jesus, and learning that he was coming to hold a mass meeting within walking distance, the boy took his lunch of five loaves and two fishes and went to see Jesus. What a choice for a boy given the numerous other choices available to him. Extrapolating from modern games that boys play, this boy could have chosen to attempt a few dunks on the basketball court, or try a few aces on the tennis court. He might have chosen to join other boys in a game of baseball or take a swim at the public swimming pool. In fact, he could have engaged in some kind of deviant behavior. Instead, he went to see Jesus, for Jesus was coming that way, and the journey must have been some distance from the boy's home because he took lunch. There is a critical need for young people with spiritual inquisitiveness, who will choose to attend a religious service rather than a basketball game.

He was focused and disciplined. His attention span for spiritual things was remarkable. This was a long meeting. All four Gospels record it. John alone identifies the boy, but Matthew, Mark, and Luke were impressed with its length. Matthew states that the miracle of the feeding of the five thousand took place "When it was evening" (Matt. 14:15). Mark reports its occurrence "When it grew late" (Mark 6:35). Luke says, "The day was drawing to a close" (Luke 9:12). Without elaborating on the freedom the Holy Spirit allows for apostolic expressions of the same event, and its meaning regarding biblical inspiration, I want to highlight the length of that mountainside open-air meeting that this boy attended all day. It lasted until the evening shadows were lengthening, the day "was drawing to a close," and the boy was still there. He was a model young man whose spiritual needs were being met by the Ruler/Teacher/Preacher. Meeting that day on the Galilean mountain were need and substance. The youth had a need, and Jesus provided the spiritual substance to satisfy that need. May that have been the reason that the multitude stayed all day? If preachers today could replicate the style and substance of the great Preacher, would believers cease complaining about length of services?

He had well-established priorities. His lunch of barley loaves and fishes was untouched until the setting sun, "The day was drawing to a close." May we assume that he placed his spiritual appetite at this time above his physical needs? Did he decide that this was the opportunity of a lifetime, so lunch could wait, because it is always available? Here is a boy who was practicing delayed self-gratification, an alien concept in this culture of instantaneity and immediacy. And he did it despite countervailing forces, not the least of which was a delicious lunch at hand.

For a boy to endure the palate-titillating aroma of freshly baked loaves and recently prepared saliva-pleasing fishes all day is a rare accomplishment. It speaks eloquently of discipline, focus, and in-place priorities. I can relate to that boy, although, at that time in my life, I was not as disciplined. As an elementary student in my homeland, Jamaica, I walked seven miles to and from school each day. Mother prepared delicious lunches from favorite Jamaican cuisine and instructed me not to touch it till noon. Often, the temptation was irresistible. Encouraged by fellow students, I disobeyed and shared in lunch-tasting escapades on the way to school.

Because the boy in our text kept his priorities straight, because he displayed delayed self-gratification, because he had an inquisitive appetite for the bread of life, thus postponing satisfaction of physical needs, his resources were available to meet a critical need on that mountain in Galilee. This generation with its appetite for instantaneous gratification, its culture of immediacy, its economics of plenty, its credit card economy that facilitates acquisition painlessly and promptly, knows very little about postponed gratification. A disturbing consequence is increasing debts and, often, irresistible temptation to acquire ill-gotten gains. Speaking as a university president, I know of the struggles students have to postpone gratification, both physical and material. Falling prey to this acquisitive culture, many misplace priorities and miss educational opportunities.

The boy was socially responsible; he was willing to share. Andrew introduced him as someone with some resources, but even Andrew was doubtful of the adequacy of five loaves and two fishes to feed that crowd. His finitude blurred his perception that the Creator was at hand. He had not heard Jesus say to Phillip, "Where are we to buy bread?" Oh, the potency of that "we," the promise it contains, the power it projects, the comfort it creates, the victory it assures, the miracles it works. One such miracle was about to take place for immediately after he was introduced to Jesus, the boy gave his lunch to the Ruler. He saw a desperate situation, a critical need, and willingly gave that which was in his hands. And that is all God asks for: "What is that in your hands?"

Because he was there and willingly presented his meager resources to Jesus, five thousand men were fed, women with babies in hands and toddlers holding onto their skirts were fed, fishermen from the sea of Tiberias, farmers from surrounding regions, and pilgrims on their way to the feast of the Passover who may have been in that crowd were fed. This boy and Jesus saved the moment. Certainly in his youth the boy displayed social responsibility, untainted altruism.

Finally, the boy displayed total commitment; he gave it all. The text says that Jesus took the loaves, not some of them, and after giving thanks, the disciples served the people, and all were fed. A truth-seeking boy disciplined with clear priorities, committed to social responsibility and sacrificial stewardship in service with Jesus, is the promise of a better world. To train such young people, society's three nurturing institutions—families, churches, and schools—must form a coalition not only of concern, but of resources to teach such values displayed in the boy with the loaves and fishes.

Influenced by ubiquitous television, radio, and other mass communication media, modern-day youth is continuously served a menu of promiscuous sex, drug consumption, misplaced priorities, and immediate self-gratification. This is a culture that erodes respect for structure and authority, and parental authority is an attendant casualty.

It is logical to assume that this boy in our story developed the qualities of spiritual appetite, self-discipline, and altruism from his parents. We are informed and challenged by the lesson here. Our children reflect parental leadership or the lack thereof.

A most critical aspect in the training of our youth is the call for total commitment. Sacrificial stewardship intensifies personal commitment and influences others. The invitation is to place all on the altar of sacrifice. And the ultimate question comes with clarion clarity, is your all on the altar of sacrifice laid?

Ruler of creation, the youth of today encounter endless and recurring forces encouraging behavior that negates traditional religious values espoused by society. Causes of most social deviancy reside in methods of education that emphasize mostly intellectual achievements. The God-man Jesus, the Christ, received an education that was holistic, intellectual, social, physical, and theological. May our families, churches, and schools provide curriculums patterned after that which educated the Son of God. With divine assistance we may train a generation of youth intellectually equipped and committed to worship God and serve where social needs exist. Amen.

Ten

SERVICE BETWEEN SABBATHS

But wanting to justify himself,
he asked Jesus, "And who is my neighbor?"

—Luke 10:29

AFTER TWO THOUSAND YEARS OF HISTORY, the Christian Church still seeks definition regarding its nature and purpose in the world. For some, the church operates like an exclusive private club restricted for the "sanctified." For others it serves primarily a social purpose with few distinguishing marks from other voluntary organizations. Still others perceive the church as an organization comprised of saints who must maintain a distance from defiling influences in the world.

There is a view, the one I espouse, which envisions the church in the world, wherever there are those souls still shackled by sin and its destructive consequences. This view is informed by the great commission of our Lord (Matt. 28:19–20; 24:14). Here the faithful are sent into all the world with a message of hope, a message delivered between Sabbaths, between services. Those who conceive of the church as a congregation of the sanctified who meet to congratulate each other and to "comfort the comforted" see no need to take the message of hope beyond the walls of the sanctuary. So, at the end of each Sabbath service, when the preacher bids good-bye and the congregation departs, church is out, out of worship, out of testifying, out of the mood to help the helpless.

In sending the church into the world, our Lord defines a gospel with social consequences. This is a world with political, economic, environmental, educational, and familial problems. The gospel of salvation is also a gospel of relevance. The ministry of Jesus epitomizes the coincidence of spiritual and social needs of people. So church is never dismissed. When congregational worship terminates, the church disperses to serve.

The tenth chapter of Luke bears a most informative message regarding the role of religion beyond the doors of the church. Responding to a lawyer's question regarding who is a neighbor, Jesus told the story of the Good Samaritan. It pertains to a man on his way from Jerusalem to Jericho who was robbed, beaten, and left seriously wounded. A priest came upon the scene of the crime and, seeing the wounded man, passed by on the other side of the road. Similarly, a Levite came along, observed the scene, saw that somebody was wounded and needed help, but went his way leaving the wounded man lying.

But a Samaritan came along, had compassion on the wounded man, attended his wounds, took him to an inn, stayed with him for a night, and paid for the cost of his stay at the inn. Then Jesus asked, "Which of these three, do you think, was a neighbor to the man who fell into the hands of the robbers?"

Beyond defining who is a neighbor, this story teaches the role of the church between Sabbaths, once worship service is over.

The priest's behavior defines service contained within the walls of the sanctuary. (See Luke 10:31.) Conceivably, he had just completed his two weeks of ministering in the temple in Jerusalem. Every year priests from parts of Palestine had to go to Jerusalem to serve for two weeks in the temple. Perhaps he had just completed his two weeks and was on his journey home by way of Jericho. Arriving unexpectedly on the gruesome scene, he was unprepared to help the wounded. For him, church was out, was dismissed. Apparently, there was no relevance between what happened in the temple and the needs of the wounded. For him, there was no service between Sabbaths, where service calls for help to the wounded, and wounds inflicted on humanity are not always physical.

Likewise, a Levite came on the crime scene, made sure that the man was wounded and passed by without giving assistance. (See Luke 10:32.) Perhaps this Levite had just completed his service in the temple, for Levites assisted priests in worship services. Perhaps both priest and Levite were leaving the same service. The priest must have left Jerusalem just before the Levite, for they came upon the same scene. It matters not whether they were just departing a worship service. The fact is, for them, church was dismissed. There was no service between Sabbaths. Religion has no relevance to a wounded world writhing in pain and suffering.

Service between Sabbaths often comes from unexpected places. The two churchmen, church officers, missed an opportunity to serve. Jesus' muted displeasure with such blatant dereliction of ecclesiastical leadership, and by inference, the lack of understanding regarding church/world relations, is introduced by the conjunction "but" (Luke 10:33). "But a Samaritan" came on the scene of the crime, had compassion, and ministered to the wounded. If the church will not serve, the stones will cry out. So, between Sabbaths, when the church fails, help to the wounded may come from where it is unexpected.

Service between Sabbaths is magnanimous service; it is service without conditions. The nationality of the wounded man remains unknown. If he was a Jew, the Samaritan's act of mercy takes on even more profound meaning, since he could not expect reciprocal behavior. Jewish disdain for the Samaritans was intense and demeaning. To touch a Samaritan was defiling. This stranger expected nothing in return for all his acts of mercy showered upon the wounded man.

Service between Sabbaths, at times, involves risk. The road between Jerusalem and Jericho has long stretches of rocky banks, deep ravines, and uninhabited hillsides. It was with extreme interest that I anticipated the trip by bus from Jerusalem to Jericho on my first visit to Israel. A lonely traveler along that road is exposed and is easy prey to robbers hiding behind those rocky banks. But the Samaritan was undaunted by dangers lurking in that neighborhood. He took his time to serve adequately. The need for service cannot wait until it is safe or convenient.

Service between Sabbaths often requires sacrifice. After staying with the wounded stranger in rented quarters that night, and before leaving the following day, the Samaritan gave two denarii to the innkeeper with a promise upon his return to pay any further costs. Two denarii was the equivalent of two days' wages in that economy. A pretty expensive investment in someone wounded and dying he had only met the day before.

Service between Sabbaths involves acts of neighborliness. Jesus told this story in response to a lawyer's question, "who is my neighbor." The neighbor of the wounded man was neither the priest nor Levite. Rather, it was the Samaritan who had compassion and extended a hand of mercy. Clearly, physical proximity does not define neighborliness. Socioeconomic similarities or club affiliations are not necessary elements in defining a neighbor. Similar racial and ethnic backgrounds, political party membership, or even common doctrinal affirmations are not grounds for neighborliness. There are just two necessary elements in a neighborly act. They are need and mercy. When compassion energizes mercy to meet a need, a neighbor is at hand.

Service between Sabbaths is anonymous service. For in God's scheme of things, it is not who you are, but how you serve that counts. In this most informative story told by Jesus, read and studied by numerous believers across the centuries, nobody knows the names of the chief actors. A certain lawyer, a certain man fell among thieves, a certain priest, a Levite, a certain Samaritan, a host at the inn—all remain nameless, for heaven regards service above salutation.

Finally, service between Sabbaths makes readiness, preparation, a prime requisite, for the opportunity to serve comes when it is least expected. Our text says, "Now by chance a priest was going down that road" (Luke 10:31a). He was unprepared theologically, for he saw no relevance between his affirmation of faith and human need. He was unprepared ecclesiastically, for benediction in the sanctuary service meant church was out, dismissed. There was, for him, accordingly, no service between Sabbaths. So he lost the opportunity to be neighborly.

On this side of paradise, the church is always on the Jericho road, east of Eden. Strewn along this highway are the wounded bodies of the neglected, the forgotten, the hungry, the abused, and the shackled with every kind of human misery. Jesus sends the church into the world with a winning and a saving message, and effective salvaging of souls takes place between Sabbaths.

Have we been able to distinguish between worship and service? We worship God, but serve men and women. The latter presents endless opportunities daily, as the meaning of worship is defined and actualized by service.

We need a new song for the Jericho road. The old song goes: On the Jericho road there is room for just two, just Jesus and you. The new song is: On the Jericho road, there is room for us three; Jesus, my neighbor, and me.

Eternal God of the entire creation, open our eyes that we may see a vineyard of service far beyond the walls of our sanctuaries of worship. Paths of our pilgrimage are strewn with wounded souls needing a touch of kindness, a word of encouragement. Lead us to see that indeed there are numerous opportunities for service between Sabbaths. And in our neighborly acts of kindness may your name be extolled and glorified. Amen.

Eleven

THE MINISTRY OF PRESENCE

Now there are varieties of gifts, but the same Spirit;

and there are varieties of services, but the same Lord;

and there are varieties of activities, but it is the same God

who activates all of them in everyone. To each is given the

manifestation of the Spirit for the common good. To one is

given through the Spirit the utterance of wisdom, and to

another the utterance of knowledge according to the same

Spirit, to another faith by the same Spirit. . . . All these are

activated by one and the same Spirit, who allots to

each one individually just as the Spirit chooses.

—1 Corinthians 12:4–9a, 11

GOD'S CHURCH IN AMERICA exists in a land of plenty. For the past decade this nation has amassed unprecedented wealth. In fact, most nations on this planet are impacted in some way by America's wealth. The economic boom is spawning multimillionaires at an alarming pace. Conspicuous consumption characterizes acquisition of goods of all kinds. The frequent question is "Aren't you better off than you were eight years ago?"

Indeed, this is a land of plenty, and the church enjoys its wealth. A great challenge for the church is not to confuse material prosperity with spiritual health, spiritual maturity, and spiritual well-being. Wealth is not an enemy of the church; rather it could be an invaluable asset in promoting God's dominion building here on this planet.

But the church has even greater assets, which, if utilized within the favorable environment it now enjoys, could become a weaver of the moral fabric of our nation. Paul in his first letter to the Corinthians speaks of the multiple gifts of the Spirit. Should these become functionally operative among communities of believers, God's church would become a mighty, conquering army in the cause of service.

One ministry that Paul did not explicitly mention but that was characteristic of the ministry of Jesus and in all effective Christian service is what I call "the ministry of presence." This ministry is simply being there with a wounded soul, offering a cup of cold water, a word of comfort, a permitting presence, a nod of understanding.

This rare ministry, this underrated service, is most dramatically displayed in the story of the Good Samaritan (Luke 10:25–37). Sometimes lost in considering the Samaritan's humanitarian compassion in contradistinction to the priest's and Levite's lack of concern for the wounded, often overshadowed by the dressing of wounds, transportation to an inn, and paying two denarii for overnight expenses, is the critical ministry the wounded man received that night. After doing all of the above, the Samaritan stayed with the wounded man that night. It was a soothing, therapeutic ministry; it was a ministry of presence.

Oh, it is easy to call the ambulance; dialing 911 takes little effort. Sending someone to help is acceptable; sending some funds to help out is good; but being there, being present, speaks eloquently of not only intense concern but of the importance and the worth of a wounded soul. Modern technology facilitates easy substitution of other means to reach those in need. E-mail is all the rage; telephones are ubiquitous; computers multiply; but the virtual church will never be an acceptable and effective substitute for the actual church. The ministry of presence has no heir apparent with promise, for the church is sent into the world where the people are.

The ministry of presence is all-inclusive, it involves pulpit and pew, and the pew outnumbers the pulpit. Everyone does not have the gifts that Paul enumerates in our text. But everyone has a presence, which is a very underused asset of the church. A presence transcends things. It establishes an I–thou, subject-to-subject relationship. Here is person responding to person. Other forms of service where things are sent to the needy—although things are frequently needed—establish an I-it relationship, where personal interaction is absent, and some aspects of psychotherapeutic healing never take place. Medical practice has recently rediscovered the therapeutic, healing power of more patient-oriented treatment. Moving from strictly social and clinical diagnosis and prescriptive approaches to the practice of medicine, physicians have rediscovered the healing power of doctor-patient interaction, where faith and belief systems play therapeutic roles. Accordingly, the chaplain is now a part of a treatment regimen for patients.

An interesting commentary on the positive effects generated by wholesome personal interaction is that married couples reportedly live longer than singles. Here I speak not as an expert, but as a keen observer of social trends.

The ultimate endorsement of the ministry of presence is that it characterizes the ministry of Jesus. At key points in his ministry, Jesus did not send a disciple; he was there. He talked with the woman of Samaria at Jacob's well; he graced the home of Jairus to heal his daughter, and while on the way, healed the woman who was sick for twelve years. On the way to Jericho, he responded to the cry of a blind man and restored his sight. At the pool of Bethesda, a man lame for thirty-eight years walked and leaped for joy because Jesus ministered unto him.

I recall an opportunity I had some years ago in the closing chapter of a pastor's ministry and life. I had been appointed president of Shaw University in Raleigh, North Carolina, and had begun visiting his church. We developed a mutually rewarding fellowship, and he intensely sought my commitment to help in keeping the flock focused after his departing this life. Word reached me that his life was ebbing fast and he desperately needed to see me. As I stood at his bedside and assured him of my assistance in keeping ablaze the beacon he had lit and kept blazing for nearly thirty years, he said, "Now, I can die in peace."

Shortly after, he joined his Lord. As I recall previous meetings with this pastor, none brings me greater joy and feelings of effective service than that farewell meeting when I blessed him with that ministry of presence.

"You may not be a leader like Peter, you may not preach like Paul, but you can tell the story of Jesus, you can say he died for all."

Forever thankful are we, dear God, for the opportunity and capacity to minister where human needs exist. May we be there with a word of hope, a permissive presence, a touch of tenderness when needed. A world of social dislocations and physical incapacities offers numerous occasions for the ministry of presence. Keep us alert and ready to serve. Amen.

PART THREE

Redemptive Human Relationships

Twelve

FATHERHOOD
Beyond Paternity

The Lord said, "Shall I hide from Abraham
what I am about to do, seeing that Abraham shall
become a great and mighty nation, and all the nations of
the earth shall be blessed in him? No, for I have chosen
him that he may charge his children and his house-
hold after him to keep the way of the Lord by doing
righteousness and justice; so that the Lord may bring
about for Abraham what he has promised him."

—Genesis 18:17–19

THROUGHOUT OUR LAND, there is a consistent cry for the reintroduc-
tion of traditional and spiritual values into transactional and personal relations. Such cardinal values as promise keeping, honesty, respect for life and limb, truth telling, responsibility, justice, and
equality have either totally disappeared from human relations or
have been relegated to remote regions of our work-a-day world.

Ethics is an alien word in our culture. During the Watergate hearings that led to the resignation of President Nixon, I was then chair
of the department of Ethics and Society at Howard University's
Divinity School. The day when H. R. Haldeman, a high official in the
Nixon White House, was to appear before the Senate committee that
was conducting the hearings, I joined the long line waiting patiently
to enter the hall of the Senate building where the hearings were held
on Capitol Hill in the nation's capital.

The waiting seemed endless. While we were waiting, a communal atmosphere developed as we shared opinions and learned particulars about each other. Word circulated that I was a professor of ethics at Howard University. Someone from the crowd approached me with this question, "Are you the professor that I heard is out of a job?"

The sinister implication in that question is a sad commentary on the low regard and the dim view that the populace has regarding the conduct of public officials in our land. In fact, for some, ethics is not an operative discipline in modern society, where "everybody does his thing." The principled guidelines of accepted conduct have largely disappeared from societal life. Those concerned with this moral drift are asking questions. How did we lose our moral compass? How may we stem this seemingly relentless slide leading to national decay and possible ultimate destruction? The sweep of history testifies to the inevitable rise and fall of powerful nations whose downfall is linked to corruption and moral decay at all levels of societal life.

Corrective measures must be inclusive. Morality may not be legislated, but when the common good involves equity and justice, legislation establishes the climate and, at times, the instruments to enforce compliance. Ecclesiastical pronouncements will not automatically effectuate moral conduct, although moral suasion by way of pulpit proclamations regarding the gospel of brotherhood may jog the conscience of the faithful. Legislation and proclamation play significant roles in establishing moral parameters and desirable ethical behavior, but compliance, effective comprehensive conformity, is marginal.

Laws intended to modify behavior elicit external compliance, but such cardinal elements of ethical behavior as motive, altruism, and intending the good of others are not necessary concomitants of coerced behavior. Doctrinal affirmations and pulpit proclamations have limited success in spawning moral actions in societal settings, because few see the relationship between beliefs and social action. The sanctuary door shuts in the church and shuts off the gospel from the world. These two institutions, church and state, play an important role in setting the tone of morality in a nation: the former by proclaiming the gospel of brotherhood, and the latter by legislating limits of personal and social behavior to avoid excesses.

Church and state are necessary but not sufficient instruments to lay the moral foundations of a nation. God has provided another way, a most effective way to teach and enforce the practice of morality. I speak of the family, a God-fearing family. Scripture declares it: "Train children in the right way, and when old, they will not stray" (Prov. 22:6). And the facts of history testify to it. Probability is high that values inculcated in early childhood and reinforced in those formative years in the home will inform and guide in later years, influencing personal and transactional relations. Indeed, the child is father of the man, as the sage declares.

I believe that a nuclear family structure involving father and mother as "priest" and "priestess" teaching and practicing religiously grounded values at home is critical to laying a moral foundation for children, and by extension the nation. Ideally, such a family would be led by a strong, faithful, and benevolent father. Single mothers do an excellent job in raising children but few would deny a preference for having a responsible and caring father of their children in the home. He would provide security, help enforce discipline, be exemplary of true manhood to a son, and assist a daughter in her quest for identity in male/female relationships.

Abraham in our text epitomizes such a father. He is a prime example of "fatherhood beyond paternity." As patriarch, prophet, priest, father of the faithful, and friend of God, Abraham earned heaven's highest praise for exemplifying paternal responsibility. Genesis 18:19 declares God's confidence and approval in this father, "No, for I have chosen him [Abraham], that he may charge his children and his household after him to keep the way of the Lord by doing righteousness and justice. . . ."

Years of faithful following yielded this unparalleled divine benediction on Abraham. Commanded to take his family and leave Ur of the Chaldees in Mesopotamia into a land yet unknown to him, Abraham departed his father's house with his wife and vast possessions (Gen. 12). At seventy-five years of age, Abraham undertook a journey of faith that brought him numerous trials. His father, Terah, died along the way. Undeterred, his caravan of animals and people confronted strange people and experienced drought that sent them to Egypt seeking help. An intense family dispute with his nephew, Lot, resulted in separation, Abraham being the peacemaker. Eventually, the caravan arrived in Canaan, the land of promise, after a fifteen-hundred-mile journey from Ur of the Chaldees.

God knew Abraham and praised him especially as a religious man who worshiped Jehovah while living in the midst of idol worshippers. Inhabitants of the city of Ur worshipped the moon god. Abraham represented a minority, albeit a minority worshipping the true God, a critical reminder that the majority is not necessarily right. He drew divine approval specifically for inculcating religious principles in his children and household, "No, for I have chosen him, that he may charge his children and his household after him to keep the way of the Lord. . . ."

Abraham's paternal responsibility in teaching his family to do justice and mercy characterized his long tedious journey. Along the way, wherever he pitched his tent he built an altar and worshipped the God of creation (Gen. 12:7; 13:18). Worship was a habit of the soul, not a hollow ritual at times of convenience. It was central to his religious leadership and for teaching his children basic values of justice and good judgment. Here is a father instructing his children regarding social responsibility and altruism, values that seem alien to our present culture. The text declares that teaching the way of the Lord to children includes sensitivity to the other, for we are our brother's keepers.

Effective teaching of children, executing this divinely sanctioned mandate, requires a fatherhood that is more than mere paternity. Fatherhood connotes all the positive characteristics expected in a functioning father. He is consistently religious, a church man, instructs his family in religiously grounded values, including concern for the common good; he is accessible to his family continually, not sporadically. He is a provider for their myriads needs and radiates love throughout his family. He is firm in administering discipline with kindness and understanding.

Fatherhood may not include paternity. Adopted children receive benefits of a stable family. Paternity is bare bone genetics. It is primarily physical. Absent fundamental characteristics of fatherhood, paternity is a curse, a bane on society. Paternity produces, but does not provide. The paternal father was there but may not now be there.

Accessibility, caring, loving, leading, committing, worshiping, and teaching religious principles constitute the recurring rituals of more than just a paternal father. Some paternity never transforms into fatherhood. Genetics and the courts may establish paternity, but never fatherhood. Paternity is purely physical, whereas fatherhood is relational.

Evidence multiplies that social pathologies of the day link directly to absentee, delinquent paternal fathers. Boys grow up without the benefits of discipline and example. Girls miss the critical opportunity to develop wholesome male/female relationships exemplified by a caring father. Some children become increasingly angry with society. They cultivate delinquency and social alienation causing deviant behavior, some of which are destructive to themselves and others.

Before becoming a victim of the ire of hard working mothers who maintain a stable, caring home from which successful children have gone to become productive Americans, let me applaud you for stepping into the breach and providing the best possible nurturing environment for your children. Successes are praiseworthy and should be appropriately recognized. However, I think that most mothers would rather have a husband who practices the elements of fatherhood to assist in establishing a stable home, thus providing the reinforcement that each legitimately brings to effective parenting.

I think that the social pathologies so prominent in America—loss of respect for authority, spousal and child abuse, untrammeled greed, dishonesty and fraud by both white- and blue-collar types, drug abuse, rage among adults and children, daily homicides, rapes, continual acts of inequities and injustice—all may be attributed, somewhat, to the loss of family values of the type taught by Abraham. There is a critical need for fatherhood as we have defined it.

The Abrahamic model of fatherhood must be introduced into our culture, our world if justice, judgment, and appropriate personal and social values must inform conduct. In no other way will this frightening moral drift be reversed. A final characteristic of fatherhood is that fathers walk the talk. Of Abraham, God said that Abraham will charge his children and household to follow God. Children could follow his standards because they were grounded in practiced religious values as he knew them. Setting standards should be reinforced with observance.

With apologies to an inspired author, I declare, "The greatest want of the world is the want of men, men who are true to duty as the needle is to the pole. Men who will call sin by its right name. Men who will stand for right though the heavens fall."[7]

> *Rise up, O men of God! Have done with lesser things;*
> *give heart and mind and soul and strength,*
>   *to serve the King of kings.*
> *Rise up, O men of God! His kingdom tarries long;*
> *Bring in the day of brotherhood and end the night of wrong.*
> *Rise up, O men of God! The Church for you doth wait,*
> *her strength unequal to her task; rise up, and make her great!*
> *Lift high the cross of Christ! Tread where his feet have trod;*
> *as brothers of the Son of man, rise up, O men of God!"Amen.*[8]

Thirteen

WORTH VERSUS WEALTH

And he said to them, "Take care! Be on your guard
against all kinds of greed; for one's life does not con-
sist in the abundance of possessions."

—Luke 12:15

The thief comes only to steal and kill and destroy. I
came that they may have life, and have it abundantly.

—John 10:10

A TELEVISION AD promoting a certain automobile declares, "Bigger is better." This phrase precisely describes the unbridled materialism dominating modern culture. Conspicuous consumption in ownership of automobiles, homes, clothes, and just things seems to be a national obsession. As the number of multimillionaires increases accompanied by their ostentatious display of luxury, those of modest means, in an effort to "keep up with the Jones," get involved in enormous debt by way of credit cards. Some even describe this as a plastic economy.

Unbridled materialism represents a massive reversal of basic human values. Priorities become displaced where things supersede people. Wealth, possessions, things help define human relations; thus one's worth, one's value, one's importance is predicated more on the material than the personal.

In times of crisis in intimate relations, the fallacy of placing possessions above people appears sometimes in most dramatic forms. The case of the fifty-dollar Porsche is informative. A California newspaper carried an ad offering a luxurious Porsche for fifty dollars. A luxurious car for fifty dollars must be junk, it was thought, so there were no responses to the ad for a long time. Out of curiosity some-one appeared at the home of the seller.

The garage door was raised, and there was a sleek, shining Porsche sitting in the garage looking as if it had never been driven. "May I drive it around the block?" the curious visitor asked. The woman presented the key and the visitor found that the Porsche drove as a new car, without any noticeable flaw. After a brief trip, the visitor asked with understandable curiosity. "This car is flawless, why fifty dollars?" The seller replied, "Let me explain. My husband ran off with his sec-retary and has run out of money. He has asked me to sell the car and send him the money, so fifty dollars."

Beyond the humor of this story lies a most critical lesson germane to the title of this sermon. When meaningful human relations disap-pear, the value, the worth of material things diminishes. That woman could have sold that luxury car for its real worth and sent her hus-band fifty dollars and kept the rest. But those funds would have been a painful reminder of a broken relationship. This story is one re-minder of the fallacy of placing ultimate value on things. At critical moments in our lives, wholesome relationships, and not the abun-dance of things, are what really prove important.

Central to the teachings of Jesus is the need for a relationship with him above and beyond the riches of the world. The great com-mandment as Jesus stated it is love to God and humankind. Here is the real love triangle, the believer's love to God and his/her love to neighbor. On this love triangle, Jesus says, hang all the law and the prophets. All scripture revolves around this basic concept of love; thus, because love is a relationship category, ultimate value or worth issues from faith relations with God, as do altruistic relations with fellow human beings.

Jesus was most emphatic in warning against overreliance on ma-terial things. "And he said to them, 'Take care! Be on your guard against all kinds of greed; for one's life does not consist of abundance in possession'" (Luke 12:15). Here Jesus separates life, a word I shall further examine, from material possessions. This is not a promising statement for our acquisitive culture, where the idea that "bigger is better" dominates.

Expanding on the ultimate grounds supporting a life worth living, Jesus again speaks: "I came that they might have life, and have it abundantly" (John 10:10b). The previous saying of Jesus separates life from the abundance of material things. In John, he promises life "more abundantly." What are the meanings of "life" and "abundance" in these two texts so basic to Christian beliefs?

In these texts, Jesus consciously uses a Greek word for life that clearly distinguishes it from mere physical existence. Greek, the original language of the New Testament, uses two different words to distinguish between physical existence and eternal life. *Bios* refers to physical, biological existence. The word biology derives from this Greek root. Wherever *bios* is used in Greek literature, it means life in the physical, earthly, temporal existence.

The other Greek word for life is *zoe*. Whenever used, it refers to life on the spiritual level; specifically, it refers to eternal life. In both texts, Jesus uses the word *zoe* as he speaks of living in the spiritual sphere. In Luke, Christ says that a person's *zoe* or eternal life does not consist of the abundance of material possessions. In John, he says he has come that you might have *zoe*, and that you might have it more abundantly. In both instances, Jesus did not use life as *bios*, for abundance in connection with *bios*, or a life on the physical plane, is quantitative; abundance in this sense speaks of things, of possessions; bigger in this instance would be better.

On the contrary, the Ruler says, "I have come that you might have *zoe*, life eternal, and that you might have it more abundantly." Here abundance relates to life on the spiritual plane. Now it is qualitative, for it describes not abundant things, but fullness and maturity in relationship between God and humankind.

Acquiring wealth is not necessarily evil. God desires that we prosper and be in health. Two of God's most faithful servants in scripture were Abraham and Job, both of whom were very wealthy. But their prosperity did not blur their heavenly vision. They were exemplary in faithful following. They did not confuse *zoe* with *bios*, that is, eternal life with mere physical existence. God gives and God takes away, says Job. He recognized that ultimate worth, ultimate significance resided in his relationship with God, and not in his massive wealth.

Punctuating the irreplaceable importance of divine/human relations in God's redemptive plan, neither Gabriel, an angel high in the hierarchy of angels, nor any other heavenly messenger was sent to earth to establish the plan of salvation. God sent God's Son, and Jesus says, "I came that they may have life, and have it abundantly." In taking our likeness, in becoming human, Jesus identifies with fallen men and women. A relationship of hope is established.

The intent of the sentence "I came" may be more effectively stated in the perfect tense, "I have come." Stated in this grammatical form, it connotes an accomplished act impacting both present and future. His coming is for all generations. There is the ring of permanence to his coming. One inspired interpreter of scripture states that in taking our bodily form and experience, Jesus has tied himself to humanity with a cord that can never be broken.

A religious experience fed by an intimate personal experience with Christ moves one from religious life on the fringes to the core of commitment and service. For faithful following transcends perfunctory ritualism, mere doctrinal affirmation, formal church membership, or plausible altruism. These may serve some purpose in the total scheme of Christian development. But these are all consequences to accepting and embracing the Christ as one's personal savior.

We are saved from a sinful past for membership in the family of God, with all the acts of worship and service attendant to membership in this family. And speaking of family, I am underscoring a relationship that exceeds mere physical existence. It is living on the *zoe* plane, where abundance is qualitative. Life at its best, life to the fullest, life reaching its maximum potentials—this is entailed in the promise of having life more abundantly.

In this promise, Jesus provides a critical corrective to the pervasive materialism of this present age. A money culture tends to feed the human proclivity for acquisitiveness. Selfish individualism dries up the milk of human kindness, and in its most extreme manifestation, relegates religious matters to a sphere of insignificance. I vividly recall a short poem recited to me by a used car salesman in Chicago many years ago. After looking at a car he showed me and deciding to visit other used car dealerships, I turned to the salesman and said I would return to purchase his car if I didn't find a better bargain.

He replied that he could not promise me that this car would be here when I return for his motto is: "Almighty dollar with the smiling face, in thee there is great power, make my pocket thy hiding place, I need thee every hour." I think that salesman articulated the motto of materialism. The almighty dollar has replaced the Almighty in numerous hearts throughout our land. Quantitative aspirations have overshadowed the qualitative values characteristic of the abundance that Jesus has promised those who receive him.

The abundant life, though primarily spiritual and qualitative in nature, does not exclude practical aspects of life on earth. Jesus is explicit regarding this. His invitation is that we accept the kingdom of heaven and all things necessary for physical existence will be given. His invitation is that we put treasure in the bank of heaven where it will last; for earthly wealth neither satisfies fully nor has lasting value.

The worth of a soul rests in the transforming relationship with Jesus. It's a relationship intended to last forever. All material possessions disappear with the fleeting wings of time. Jesus is real and has promised to be with the faithful always.

In Jesus, I become a member of the family of God, so I can sing:

My Father is rich in houses and land;
He holdeth the wealth of the world in His hands,
Of rubies and diamonds, of silver and gold,
His coffers are full, He has riches untold.
I'm a child of the King,
With Jesus my Savior, I'm a child of the king."[9]

Ultimate worth is relationship with God, who is ultimate.

Fourteen

LOVE
The Perfect Triangle

He answered, "You shall love the Lord your God with all your
heart, and with all your soul, and with all your strength, and with
all your mind; and your neighbor as yourself."

—Luke 10:27

Beloved, let us love one another, because love is from God;
everyone who loves is born of God and knows God.
Whoever does not love does not know God, for God is love.

—1 John 4:7–8

TINA TURNER, THE CELEBRATED SINGER, asks "What's love got to do with it?" If she is speaking about human relations, which the lyrics of that song clearly reference, then my response is "Love has everything to do with it."

Love is one of the most abused, misunderstood, and loosely used words in our vocabulary. For whether it is Stevie Wonder's song "I Just Called to Say I Love You" or Diana Ross and the Supremes' plea to "Stop! In the Name of Love," all seem to define love in purely sentimental overtones. These songs are sung by celebrated artists and titillate our capacity to enjoy the beauty of melody and the sentimental lure of the opposite gender, but the essence of love, especially Christian love, is absent from these superbly sung lyrics.

A full understanding of love convinces us that it is the most important principle for harmonious human relations whether this involves family, friendships, social relations, or devotion to God. If we applied love deliberately and consistently in human relations, our world would replicate the idyllic state of affairs that scripture described in Eden before disobedience to God disrupted the perfect triangle that is love to God and neighbor.

Given the present state of affairs in our world characterized by brokenness, rugged individualism, selfishness, road rage, parental delinquency, youth violence, disrespect for life and limb, incorrigible prejudice, countless unwanted children, and national stockpiles of nuclear agents of mutual destruction, to name only a few of the personal and societal pathologies that afflict the human race, it seems idle to conceive of a world where the "lion and the lamb could lie down together" and harmony would prevail.

Yet love, as is defined in this sermon, when it becomes the operational principle in human relations, serves as a catalyst for wholeness, inclusiveness, kindness, and a corrective to the brokenness between humans and God. Idealistic, indeed, but we are saved by hope.

One reason for the misuse of the word love among English-speaking individuals is its use to express a plethora of human emotions and sentiments. Whether the intent is to express sexual love or love for family, friend, or God, the English language provides just one word, whereas the Greek language provides three words that speak denotatively and precisely in efforts to express different kinds of love relationships.

The Greek word *eros* expresses love between the sexes. A physical love, it denotes intense passion, sentimental desire, uncoerced intuitive attraction for the opposite sex. The Supremes' song might be more precisely rendered "Stop! In the Name of *Eros*." *Eros* might be the most used word, for humans, with unrehearsed ease, and often without serious intent say, "I love (*eros*) you." And *eros* does not appear in scripture.

Philia defines another kind of love. As the most common word for love in Greek, it expresses affectionate regard for others. It is love within a family, a husband's love for his wife or the wife's love for her husband, children's affection for parents, or friendship among neighbors. *Philia* represents a cherished friendship, tender relations. But *philia* is prejudicial and exclusive. To be loved and cherished, one must be found among the accepted, the revered, the "club"; it is, therefore, intentional. Used in scripture (Matt. 10:37; John 11:3, 36) this word expresses a beautiful relationship.

Agape is the most common word for love in the Bible. It appears 120 times in the New Testament and represents the essence of New Testament ethics. Whereas *eros* denotes more passion than love, and *philia* is prejudicial and exclusive, *agape* is inclusive and demands the exercise of the whole person. Words commonly used for love express emotions and deal with the heart. They express experience that comes to us unsought.

But *agape* elevates love to a higher level. "*Agape* is the greatest of all virtues, the characteristic virtue of the Christian faith."[10] As the highest level of human relationships, *agape* moves from mere emotions to a guiding principle in ethical behavior. Although inclusive of emotions and appeals of the heart, it primarily involves the mind. It operates on the level of the will. Thus one does not "fall in love," implying a passive state of being where the will is dormant. Falling in love could place one in an untenable fix where the fall is for someone that is not even liked.

As the apex of both social and spiritual relations, *agape* evokes and summons numerous responses from the faithful.

It commands the improbable: "You shall love your neighbor and hate your enemy. But I say to you, Love your enemies and pray for those who persecute you" (Matt. 5:43–44). This is strange doctrine to those who believe in the eye-for-an-eye view of human relations. Reduced to mere passion and emotions, it is improbable to love your enemies. The heart cannot be commanded or coerced; it can only be nurtured and wooed.

Jesus' "strange" teachings to those trained in a tradition of retributive justice makes sense when the oxymoronic "love your enemies" defines love as an operative principle, a deliberate decision of the will. Here the believer is summoned to act even when such action defies feelings or emotions. So "love your enemies, bless them that curse you, do good to those who hate you." In this revolutionary doctrine, words like bless, do good, pray for those who despitefully use you, are clear definitions of love. Love is as love does. Love serves the highest good of the other. William Barclay states that love (*agape*) as an operative principle "is a conquest, a victory, an achievement."[11]

Love thus becomes the catalyst in that ideal triangular relationship among God, the believer, and one's neighbor. "For God so loved the world that he gave his only Son . . ." (John 3:16). "You shall love the Lord your God with all your heart, and with all your soul, and with all your strength, and with all your mind; and your neighbor as yourself" (Luke 10:27). Here is the Christian love triangle: God's love for humanity, the believer's love for God, and love of neighbor.

As the catalyst, as the operative principle in a believer's worldview, love is nonprejudicial. It is the Samaritan exerting compassion to a wounded stranger on the Jericho road. It is inclusive, for as God's goodness extends to the just and unjust, everyone, especially those wounded along life's way, needs our compassion. It is nonjudgmental, for those of us without sin may not cast the first stone. But love is in the service of truth, and as a parent applies corrective measures, which at times are punitive, to children, the faithful are exhorted by Paul to "speak the truth in love" to the wayward (Eph. 4:15).

Love is pragmatic; it spawns acts of kindness that demonstrate the nobler dimensions of the human spirit. A white teacher watched her student, a black boy, at play and saw his fruitless efforts to catch a football that should be easily caught under normal circumstances. His repeated failure brought about the following conversation between teacher and student. "Why do you fail to catch those easily thrown balls, John?" (This is a true story that took place in North Carolina, but I am using the name John to preserve anonymity.) John replied, "I can't, ma'am, because I am on dialysis." Moved with compassion, this teacher made a decision with lifelong consequences for her and John. After long discussions with her family, despite all possible overtones, this teacher decided to give John one of her kidneys. Surprise, disbelief, relief, hope, gratitude all overwhelmed John's mother when she received the news. Could such an act of compassion, uncoerced and unsolicited, transpire between two Americans of different ethnicity in a country still lashed with the whip of racial prejudice? Is there one still walking the Jericho road willing to risk life and limb to minister to a wounded boy?

Yes, there is one, a white teacher, who is stopping by to give a portion of her life to her student, a little black boy slowly dying from a failing kidney. Medical tests proved compatibility between organ donor and recipient, and the greatly anticipated day arrived. In one operating room lay a white woman, a modern good Samaritan. In another lay a black boy, the "wounded." Both surgical procedures were successful.

But there is soul-searching spiritual and practical drama to this "strange" act of human compassion. As surgeons walked from the room of the donor with a life-giving organ in hand to the room of the recipient, they were metaphorically breaking down more walls than that dividing those hospital rooms. The wall of selfishness disappeared; the wall of racial prejudice dissolved; the wall of fear for personal health dissipated; the wall of apprehension regarding societal disapproval vanished; the bridge of love between donor and recipient was permanently established. Love removes walls of separation.

John and his teacher are back in school. As she watches him play football and catch balls with unagonizing ease, as he interacts with students without pain, as he holds up his hands in her class to answer a question, his teacher, his "savior," looks at him as an extension of her life. This is compassion with a personal, permanent place in the annals of human kindness.

The teacher in this true story is a prime representative of *agape* love in action. She was not motivated by *eros*, because student John is not her lover. Neither is *philia* a prime factor, for John is not a close friend or an immediate family member. Responses to these types of love are expected, intuitive, and prejudicial. Jesus declares that when we do favors for brethren, friend, and family, the nearest and the dearest, our deeds do not exceed those of nonbelievers (Matt. 5:47).

But in this story the teacher stepped outside the close circle of friends and lovers, and by an objective, deliberate decision of the will gave a portion of her life to a needy soul, without beneficial expectations or reciprocal gestures. That's *agape* in action. This is the love our world needs—a love that loves the unlovable; a love blind to distinctions and differences. Is it possible to think of a world where the perfect love triangle defines all human relations? Oh, the prospect pleases.

Dear God, infuse within us that true love—the highest of all Christian virtues—the foundation of Christian ethics that elevates our desire, devotion, and actions above the selfish, prejudicial, and exclusive, thereby completing the perfect love triangle of God, self, and neighbor. Amen.

Fifteen

THE WISDOM OF SOLOMON
Making Difficult Ethical Decisions

God gave Solomon very great wisdom, discernment,
and breadth of understanding as vast as the sand on the
seashore, so that Solomon's wisdom surpassed the wisdom
of all the people of the east, and all the wisdom of Egypt.

—1 Kings 4:29–30

LIVING IS A SUCCESSION of decisions informed by belief systems. Some decisions are difficult since the options are unclear. In such cases, the burden to decide the right, good, or appropriate requires analysis of the situation and reflection on what is possible.

Indeed, Christian ethics seeks the best possible good for humans. But the highest good must be informed always by what is possible. Here pragmatism converts idealism into realism, and ethical decisions do not produce the right, which is dictated by a legal code, or the good, which is predetermined. Rather, such decisions may be defined as the appropriate, since analysis and reflection search for what is possible.

Making difficult decisions poses a problem for the notion of Christian perfection, if perfection denotes flawlessness, absence of error, pristine clarity among options, and strict compliance to an ethical code with predetermined decisions. So much emotional pain and depressing feelings of guilt would believers avoid, should the dynamics of making difficult decisions be understood.

Two parents in London, the medical profession, and the British Court, recently struggled with a difficult decision. The parents involved had twin baby girls joined such that one heart was sustaining both babies. Medical examination determined that one baby was a "parasite" being kept alive by the heart of the other.

It was medically determined that one heart could not keep both babies alive, and that early surgery was necessary to ensure that one of the twins would survive. And the most viable of the twins was the one to whom the heart really belonged, and to save her life the other surviving as a "parasite" had to be removed. Of course, this meant certain death.

The following ethical dilemma develops. In the first place, the code says, "You shall not murder." Yet in this case, death is inevitable either by surgery to save one, or just leaving both to die. The attending doctors suggest surgery. The parent's love for both recoils from the spectacle of death for either one. In the absence of clear, unambiguous guidance, what general principle may inform an appropriate decision? The code says it is wrong to kill. The good or acceptable end would be to keep both alive. Neither is operative in this difficult case. What is the appropriate decision?

As a historical event played out in England, an appeal was made to a "neutral" and higher authority, the British Court. Emotionally involved, the parents refused surgery. Professionally committed to save life, the doctors insisted on surgery. The courts ruled in favor of surgery, arguing that the inevitability of death for both twins without it and the possibility of saving one by surgery make this the appropriate decision.

It is now reported that both parents love and adore the surviving twin. Sometimes passion, here the love of parents, and professional commitment, here doctors' oath to save life, may predetermine difficult decisions. The courts examining this case more objectively and dispassionately made a decision for the saving of a life. The saving of a viable life informed this decision.

I propose that in most difficult situations, love should be the motivating principle. King Solomon of Israel skillfully brought this principle to bear on a difficult situation. Declared the wisest man in the eastern world (1 Kings 4:29–30), King Solomon had his wisdom put to the test.

The story appears in 1 Kings 3:15–28. Each of two women living in the same house had a son. On a certain night, one son died, and on the morrow the woman with the dead son on her bosom claimed that the other woman, now with the living child, had switched sons during the night. Her story declared that the other woman's child had died and she placed the dead child on her bed and snatched her son who was alive. So she beseeched the king to help have her child returned.

A bitter argument ensued, each woman claiming the living child. Solomon's wisdom was put to the test. "Bring me a sword," said the king, and "divide the living boy in two; then give half to the one, and half to the other."

The text says, "Because compassion for her son burned within her," the woman to whom the living child really belonged said, "Give her the living boy; certainly do not kill him!" Love for her son denounced a slaughter, while the other woman declared, "It shall be neither mine nor yours; divide it" (1 Kings 3:26).

This second woman's was a callous, loveless, hateful statement. Seizing the moment, Solomon ruled, "Give the first woman the living boy; do not kill him. She is the mother" (verse 27). The mother who refused to see her son killed rightly received the living child.

Here, King Solomon confronts a difficult situation. Absent a corroborating testimony, and pressed by two conflicting accounts, the king sought a resolution by way of analysis, reflection, and wisdom. Indeed, the real mother would rather see her son reared by another than consent to his death.

In this moment of ambiguity, the true ethical decision was made by the mother of the living son. It was a decision informed and undergirded by love. And Solomon ruled after seeing love in action.

Love, as *agape*, wills the highest good for others. For some, it might not be the "right" decision. For others, it may not be the "good" decision. But for the decision-maker, it is the "appropriate" decision, for love is the guiding principle of action.

St. Augustine advises to love God and do what you please. Although influenced by what is possible in ambiguous situations, St. Augustine's advice is not purely situational, because love for God carries its own constraints. God-likeness attends every action.

Human finitude and its attendant limitation of knowledge often prevent us from knowing all the facts. But act we must, for living is a series of actions. Refusal to act may deny another needed service and may even be disobedience to the divine mandate "Love one another."

Ethical decisions in difficult, ambiguous contexts are really not choices between good and evil. Rather, they are choices of lesser evil that may produce the greatest possible good.

This information age has complicated the process of decision making by providing a wider range of choices. Medical science and technology, for instance, have redefined the meaning of death.

Is death cerebrally determined, that is, is one dead when the brain ceases to function while the heart still beats, or must both the pulmonary and the cerebral (heart and brain) cease to function before one is declared dead? This question is now germane, because life-sustaining machines can keep the heart going even when one is in a prolonged coma.

Then the ethical question, should a loved one exhaust resources to keep one breathing artificially, hoping for a miraculous cure? Is pulling the life-sustaining plug, often called "passive euthanasia," ethically wrong? Whether a loved one exhausts all resources to keep the comatose in extended misery, hoping for a miracle, or approves cessation of the use of artificial means, thus opting for the quality rather than the quantity of life, the ethical decision is determined by motive and love.

If the intent is for the ultimate good of the other, if love informs and drives such action, then it is neither right nor good. It is appropriate action, affectionately conceived and pragmatically driven, in full surrender to the will of God and love for neighbor.

A faith driven by love of God and love of neighbor never recoils from difficult decisions. Rather, by seeking divine wisdom to reflect upon and analyze the problem at hand in quest of the best possible good for others, faith decides, and grace engenders confidence that God's will prevails and humanity is served. For in all obedient action, we are still saved by hope.

Refusal to act when confronted by difficult decisions is, in fact, an act. Such behavior may be tantamount to disobedience, cowardice, indecisiveness, resulting in loss of an opportunity to serve the good for someone. Do not wait until all the facts are in. That may never occur. Step forward in faith. God's will and someone's need may be served.

Our God of wisdom, compassion, grace, and love, life presents us with difficult decisions as we traverse this territory, East of Eden. Often what is right and good defies our finite and limited knowledge. So inspire us by the Holy Spirit to be guided by love as a controlling principle in social relations. May your will prevail, and human needs be served. Amen.

PART FOUR

Hope:

The Reason for Living

Sixteen

THE GOSPEL OF INCLUSIVENESS

> *Now all the tax collectors and sinners*
> *were coming near to listen to him. And the*
> *Pharisees and the scribes were grumbling and*
> *saying, "This fellow welcomes sinners and eats*
> *with them." So he told them this parable: . . ."*

—Luke 15:1–3

THIS FIFTEENTH CHAPTER OF LUKE utilizes a method used most effectively by Jesus in his teaching ministry. He taught by parables. Parables are stories or allegories employing practical experiences to convey spiritual lessons. Simple and uncomplicated in structure, they portray profound truths that etch themselves indelibly in minds searching for understanding.

Luke presents three parables that portray three categories of sinners and the redemptive potency of the gospel in reaching souls in any state of sin. The self-righteous Pharisees and punctilious scribes accused Jesus of associating with publicans and sinners. Their accusation essentially criticized him for accomplishing the mission for which he emptied himself of the prerogatives of deity and became man on a mission of mercy.

Jesus spoke three parables that describe three states of the unsaved and the redemptive inclusiveness of his ministry. His muted message to his critics, to these messengers of self-righteousness, is that they had placed themselves beyond God's redemptive plan, for Jesus came to save sinners and not the righteous.

Parable of the Lost Sheep. One sheep wanders from the herd of one hundred and gets lost in the wilderness. The herd is incomplete without it. The shepherd leaves the ninety-nine and searches for the one lost "until he finds it." The search is incomplete until the lost is found. He carries the sheep on his shoulders, rejoicing. Carrying the sheep means that grace does it all. We do not work our way into salvation. Lost souls are recipients of grace, not producers of it.

Redeeming the lost is an occasion for rejoicing. Friends and neighbors are called. Festivities and celebration take place, for the lost is found. Jesus punctuates the significance of one soul that is saved: "Just so, I tell you, there will be more joy in heaven over one sinner who repents than over ninety-nine righteous persons who need no repentance" (Luke 15:7). Implied here is that there is no rejoicing over those Pharisees and scribes that separate themselves from sinners and feel no need for repentance.

Parable of the Lost Coin. A woman has ten pieces of silver. One is lost in her house. A search ensues, and the method of searching differs from the search for the lost sheep. She lights a candle and sweeps the house and searches "diligently" until she finds it. This lost coin represents a different category of unsaved souls. Lost in the house means they are in close proximity—a family member, a neighbor, a social club associate, a church member—a proximity that blurs perception and dulls sensitivity.

A candle must be lit; an enhanced sensitivity is necessary to see beyond familial connections and friendly favors. The temptation is to "baptize" and make acceptable faults and failures in family and friends that we deplore in others. The candle of awareness to sharpen perception is necessary, for the inanimate coin, like the unregenerate soul, is unaware of its lost status and needs to be sought and found by the enlightened searcher.

Searching for this lost coin that does not know that it is lost requires reinforced diligence. While the lit candle enlightens the seeker and identifies the site, the seeker will "sweep the house, and search carefully until she finds it" (Luke 15:8). To save souls symbolized by a lost coin demands evangelistic skills and spiritual awareness (lit candles), focused thoroughness (sweeping the house), and sustained diligence.

But there is hope, for the coin is found and joy and celebration are shared with friends and neighbors. The value of ten pieces of silver is diminished quantitatively and qualitatively when one piece is lost, for here the whole is more than a sum of its parts. When a soul is salvaged from sin, the circle of love and fellowship becomes complete, and heaven rejoices.

The Lost Son: The Prodigal. This parable introduces a qualitatively different category of sinners, those who deliberatively and consciously choose to walk the path of disobedience and self-destruction. The younger of two sons, driven by the restlessness and irrational passion of youth, secured his portion of his father's wealth and hurriedly left home. Seeking anonymity in order to unleash a life of profligacy and unfettered debauchery, he journeyed to a far country. Luke says that in that distant land "he squandered his property in dissolute living" (Luke 15:13). Inevitably, the fool from his money will depart.

Slipping to the bottom of the socioeconomic ladder, he fed and dined with swine. His mother's tears followed him; his father's love longed for his return; his seat around the dining table remained vacant; his room remained empty. The circle of love was broken, for this son was lost.

The unique quality in the parable of the prodigal is freedom of choice. He chose to leave home, and he can choose to return. No shepherd went to the wilderness to seek him; no candle was lit, no sweeping or diligent search was made for him. Scripture says that "He came to himself" (verse 17). Conceivably, the Holy Spirit reached him in the pig pen and reminded him of his pedigree, his history, his waiting father.

Responding to that pricking of conscience, this young man in humility returned home, receiving a jubilant welcome and a symbol of renewed status, a ring on his finger. Here, regeneration and reclamation are complete. He was lost, now he is found; one is not partially found. Salvation brings about completeness.

Why did Jesus use three stories to teach the simple truth that his mission was to save the lost, and that one soul is so precious in God's dominion that he/she is earnestly sought and when found brings great joy? I believe that the three parables describe three kinds of sinners, with insightful approaches to reclaim them for God's dominion.

The coin was lost and did not know that it was lost, but it was lost anyway. Enlightened, thorough and diligent search is required to awaken and save this soul. The sheep was lost, and knew that it was away from the herd, but could do nothing about it. Salvation here came from a searching shepherd. There are those shackled and sinking in sin while nurturing a desire to change but who need a shepherd, a witness, an invitation that says this is the way; walk therein.

And then, there is the prodigal, with that precious freedom of choice. He chose to get lost in a far country, chose to be a spendthrift, chose riotous living, choices that took him to the fringes and husks of life. Memory of his past, recalling the contrast of fabulous living at home to the pig pen, brought him to his senses. He arose from the filth and garbage of the far country and went back to forgiveness, to love and service.

These three parables present the human condition in its fallen state across the sweep of history. Each shackled soul since human existence east of Eden falls into one of these categories: agonized ignorance, lost but knowing not the way of salvation (the lost sheep), the state of a seared conscience, which is impervious on its own to the pleadings of the Holy Spirit (the lost coin), or the condition of an awakened conscience pushed by physical and spiritual depravity and pulled by memory of the past (the lost son).

In each lost condition, the long arm of God's grace reaches the shackled soul with the hope of salvation. Inclusiveness defines God's rescue mission played out in the life of Christ.

God does care. God's love reaches us in any state of our being. Whether in a moral stupor (the coin), a confused awareness (the lost sheep), or heightened self-consciousness (the prodigal), states of brokenness with God in each case, souls may be redeemed. The church is sent into the world to urge them to come.

Redeemed! how I love to proclaim it!
Redeemed by the blood of the Lamb;
Redeemed, thru His infinite mercy,
His child, and forever I am,
Redeemed and so happy in Jesus,
No language my rapture can tell;
I know that the light of His presence
With me doth continually dwell.[12]

Seventeen

MORAL IMPERATIVES
OF CHRISTIAN EDUCATION

And Jesus increased in wisdom and in years,
and in divine and human favor.

—Luke 2:52

ASSESSMENT OF EFFECTIVE MINISTRY and successful stewardship utilizes varied criteria. For some, homiletic wizardry is the ultimate criterion for effective pastoral leadership. Pulpit committees searching for pastors are often swayed by "powerful preaching." Others evaluate a vibrant church by the organizing ability of church leaders. Still others rave over large congregations and sizable budgets. Seldom is the vitality of a church ministry measured by its commitment to Christian education where teaching and learning are primary means and ends in spiritual development.

In Jesus' celebrated commission to the disciples, and thus to the church, he exhorts: "Go therefore and make disciples of all nations, baptizing them in the name of the Father and of the Son and of the Holy Spirit, and teaching them to obey everything that I have commanded you. And remember, I am with you always, to the end of the age" (Matt. 28:19–20).

The church is commissioned to be a teaching institution. Sensational preaching, worshipful rituals, monetary stewardship and missionary outreach are all necessary activities for a functioning church. But they are not sufficient for a church expecting to remain alive and influential in a world steeped in an information syndrome.

Christ's was a teaching ministry. Sitting on that scenic Galilean mountainside, possibly overlooking the placid Sea of Galilee,

Matthew says that "he began to speak, and taught them, saying . . ." (Matt. 5:2). Teaching was a major instrument in simplifying profound truths for the uninitiated, and as the disciples looked on they learned from the Master Teacher how to inform and win souls for the kingdom.

Christian education takes two approaches on a church's agenda. It prepares the saints to mature both spiritually and intellectually. It also equips the faithful to be ready to defend the tenets of their beliefs. A mere emotional response to the Word dissipates when the heat of inevitable adversity surrounds the believer.

Imperatives of Christian education have particular relevance to the youth in our congregations. Modernity provides the young with uninhibited, unabashed, sensational excitement that challenges the traditional values of religious experience. An ethic of libertarianism rules the day. A permissive environment that erodes the hallmarks of acceptable conduct endorses, it seems, every iconoclast of revered mores.

Our youth are caught in this morass of ethical anarchy. As they go, so go the church and our world of tomorrow. Preaching to them is important. But teaching them fundamental elements of the Gospel and emphasizing the consequences of behavior are necessary and effective. Early intervention in the educational process is essential. Jesus affirmed this as reported in Mark 10:14. "Let the little children come to me; do not stop them; for it is to such as these that the kingdom of God belongs." Openness, humility, innocence, vulnerability, willingness to learn, and teachability are characteristics of a childhood conducive to learning. Early childhood education is essential not only in secular educational institutions, but also in church schools where religious values are woven into a liberal arts curriculum.

Four irreplaceable imperatives inherent in the "holistic" model of Christian education appear in the curriculum that guided the development of Jesus. Luke 2:52 states, "And Jesus increased in wisdom and in years, and in divine and human favor." Here is comprehensive development, total immersion in disciplines of vertical and horizontal dimensions.

Jesus increased in years (physically). His parents saw to it that all elements necessary for healthy, physical growth were included in his daily regimen. He had adequate time for relaxation and rest. Carpentry did not consume all of his time. Computers and television were not around to compete with those critical moments for rest, and if they were, Mary and Joseph, being responsible parents, would not allow it. Adequate rest is absolutely necessary for physical well-being, intellectual alertness, and temperamental equilibrium.

Health and physical development depend largely on a healthful diet. A popular saying states that garbage in, garbage out. Numerous diseases and illnesses are caused by debilitating habits and unwholesome foods that constitute the daily fare of millions. As early as 400 B.C.E., Hippocrates, known as the father of medicine, linked diet and diseases. He stated, "Let food be your medicine, and let medicine be your food. Each one of the substances of a person's diet acts upon his body and changes it in some way, and upon those changes his whole life depends." A recent popular magazine promoting healthful foods endorses Hippocrates by stating that nine thousand scientific studies have documented that food is our best medicine. The boy, Jesus, grew in years because his diet enhanced healthy development.

Luke says that Jesus increased in wisdom (intellectually). Learning from scripture, nature, and at his mother's knee, the child grew intellectually. Wisdom is the crystallization of knowledge and experience applied pragmatically. Knowledge is the prior requirement to wisdom. Jesus did not rely on pure emotion, as some do in efforts to preach. He had the facts. At twelve years of age, he astonished the intellectuals of the day, the doctors and scribes, in the temple. Luke states that "All who heard him were amazed at his understanding and his answers" (Luke 2:47). In preaching and teaching God's word, it is presumptuous to expect the Spirit to bring to remembrance what intellectual laziness prevented us from learning. The Apostle Paul exhorts the diligent study of the Word. "Do your best to present yourself to God as one approved by him, a worker who has no need to be ashamed, rightly explaining the word of truth" (2 Tim. 2:15). The incoherent emotionalism that characterizes a great deal of preaching in many pulpits of the day deprives waiting congregations of the "meat" of the Word so necessary for growth in theological understanding.

Jesus grew socially. The text says he increased in "human favor" (Luke 2:52). Rapport with human beings is a prerequisite for witnessing to them. The church is sent into the world with the message of salvation and hope. Knowledge of the times, of social and political movements, of human needs and aspirations is absolutely crucial for effective proclamation. Jesus was also a psychologist, for he knew what was in humans. Conveyors of the Word need credibility and the ability to be relevant. Someone declared that preachers should have the Bible in one hand and the newspapers in the other.

Jesus increased theologically. He increased "in divine favor" (verse 52). He knew that he should be about his Father's business. His meat was to do the will of God. That was his persuasion, passion, and purpose. Growth in the knowledge of God is the crowning principle of Christian education.

Any comprehensive curriculum designed for religious education contains these four imperatives: physical, intellectual, social, and theological disciplines. It aims for the development of the whole person. Someone states that "Christian education is the harmonious development of the physical, mental, and spiritual powers." It is harmonious development because training of the hands alone produces an automaton; educating the heart alone produces a zealot; educating the head alone yields a villain. Educate all three and there is a person prepared to live creatively in this world in preparation for the world to come.

Stakes are high, expectations exceed the ordinary, and preparation of this well-educated person, given the less demanding criteria of secular education, seems implausible. But God has given us three institutions, which, if working cooperatively, can achieve this noble goal. I speak of the Christian family, the Christian church, and the Christian college. Positive reinforcement by each will ensure the education of spiritual giants who become positive role models in social and political settings, and compelling, convincing witnesses of the Word.

Education is high on the national agenda. Families complain about the poor quality of student performance. The number who pass national tests are fewer than desirable. Never or seldom, however, do complaints about the quality of American education pertain to acceptable values or character development. Focus is almost exclusively on the cerebral, rarely on the attitudinal, where values are primary. Consequently, rugged individualism and the ethic of selfishness reign.

Given the aforementioned paradigm of holistic education, how should the state of American education be assessed? What difference in the moral element of our country would emanate from a holistic approach to education?

Christian education appropriately conceived and effectively executed will help reverse the drift to social anarchy and religious insensitivity. Christian education provides a promising answer, for its curriculum seeks to prepare citizens who are physically fit, intellectually sophisticated, socially responsible, religiously informed, and committed to do God's will. With such an attitude of receptivity to divine guidance, souls can sing:

Open my eyes, that I may see
Glimpses of truth thou hast for me.
Place in my hands the wonderful key
That shall unclasp, and set me free.
Silently now I wait for thee,
Ready, my God, thy will to see;
Open my eyes, illumine me, Spirit divine!

Open my ears, that I may hear
Voices of truth thou sendest clear;
And while the wave-notes fall on my ear,
Ev'rything false will disappear.
Silently now I wait for thee,
Ready, my God, thy will to see;
Open my ears, illumine me, Spirit divine!

Open my mouth, and let me bear
Gladly the warm truth ev'rywhere;
Open my heart, and let me prepare
Love with Thy children thus to share.
Silently now I wait for thee.
Ready, my God, thy will to see;
Open my heart, illumine me, Spirit divine! Amen.[13]

Eighteen

ON BECOMING SOMEBODY

But Jesus said, "Someone touched me;
for I noticed that power had gone out of me."

—Luke 8:46

And Jesus said, Somebody hath touched me:
for I perceive that virtue is gone out of me.

—Luke 8:46 KJV

IN SHAKESPEARE'S *Hamlet Prince of Denmark,* Hamlet, standing in the presence of fair Ophelia and experiencing the pangs of melancholy over the death of his father, recited lines oft quoted across the years that raise the ultimate question of life's meaning:

> *To be, or not to be, that is the question.*
> *Whether 'tis nobler in the mind to suffer*
> *The Slings and arrows of outrageous fortune,*
> *Or to take up arms against a sea of troubles*
> *And by opposing end them. To die: to sleep,*
> *No more; and by a sleep to say we end*
> *The heart-ache and the thousand natural shocks*
> *That flesh is heir to: 'tis a consumation devoutly to be wish'd!*[14]

For Hamlet, the death of his father seemed to have removed all meaning to life, and the incestuous relation between his uncle, now king, and his mother deepened his pain and agony.

Beyond the temporality of Hamlet's question lies life's ultimate question: what is the reason for living? Is there meaning beyond sunrises and sunsets that stretch into months and years, such times punctuated by a relentless quest for material acquisition, personal promotion, and all the ambivalent vicissitudes that define life on this planet? That, I declare, is the substantive question that lies beyond Hamlet's soliloquy, "To be or not be, that is the question."

This quest for meaning and certainty stretches across the ages and expresses itself in the myriad religions humankind has embraced. Some have found religion empty regarding this profound question of the meaning of existence. Robert Ingersoll, the celebrated atheist, reportedly stood at the graveside of his brother and cried out in great grief: "Life is a narrow vale between the cold and barren peaks of two eternities; we strive in vain to look beyond the heights; we cry aloud, and the only answer is the echo of our wailing cry."[15]

The answer to this agelong question lies in an informed perception of who and whose we are. The title of this sermon, "On Becoming Somebody," posits a Christian perspective on the quest for meaning and substance in our earthly sojourn. The search for meaning is healthy because it leads to greater understanding of God's designs for God's children. But our quest must peruse the real source of divine revelation, the scriptures.

Life's meaning is inextricably tied to self-perception, which pursues varied paths to its goal. And the ultimate goal of self-realization is to be known as "somebody" where somebody in popular parlance connotes stardom, celebrity, importance, a V.I.P. Paths usually taken to this status of "somebody" include amassing great wealth, holding positions of power, achieving the apex of professional progression, or just being the most popular person in town.

As a boy growing up on my father's farm in Jamaica, West Indies, I prayed for the days when I would go off to college and achieve the status of somebody. And, of course, the symbols of success are well known: college degrees, high-salaried position, most expensive car around, tailored high-quality suits, and a mansion on a hill overlooking the white sand beaches of Montego Bay, Jamaica.

These constituted the paths and symbols of my material understanding of "On Being Somebody" until one day Jesus was passing by in a spirit-filled, mind-informing, heart-convicting, confession-evoking, Bible-preaching worship service when the preacher said, speaking of Jesus, "I am the vine, you are the branches. Those who abide in me and I in them bear much fruit, because apart from me you can do nothing" (John 15:5). In extending the meaning of this text I declare that without Jesus I can do nothing because I am nothing, nobody.

Becoming somebody in the economy of heaven necessitates the transforming touch of the Man of Galilee. That touch transforms our scheme of values, establishes new sterling priorities, lifts our vistas of possibilities, establishes hope, where before earthly pursuits seemed like cyclical routines leading nowhere. The touch of faith gives meaning to living. It transforms our status, making us members of the family of God.

Our text quotes Jesus saying, "Somebody touched me" (Luke 8:46). This eighth chapter of Luke describes the itinerary of a busy preacher. Jesus had just returned from the country of the Garasenes across the Sea of Galilee where he had just made a madman sane. He returned to find a vast crowd waiting. Tidings of the success of his comprehensive ministry permeated the Galilean country. People heard and responded, as they will when persuasive, spirit-filled, informative, and heart-warming evangelistic preaching takes place.

In that waiting crowd was Jairus, an officer of the synagogue, who reverently besieged Jesus to visit his house to heal his only daughter. Responding to the officer's request, as he does to every sincere soul who cries out for help, Jesus was mobbed by the multitude (verse 42). It was a motley crowd including believers, truth-seekers, the sick seeking healing, conceivably some spies (scribes and Pharisees), the curious, and some just standing by. Yes, they were all there.

But there was one, a sick, sallow, weak, penniless, self-defacing woman, emaciated by twelve years of illness that local physicians had failed to heal, although they had consumed all her funds, and in those days social medicine, Medicare, and Medicaid were unavailable. Energized by this one instance of hope in him who calmed the storm, cast out devils, and made the blind see, this frail woman resolved that just a touch of his garment would make her whole.

But how could she penetrate such a motley crowd that the scripture says "pressed in on him?" Confronted by life and death questions and fueled by faith, humans do imponderable feats. This was one of those instances when feebleness and faith found a way. Pressing by the curious, the spies, the faithless seekers, passing by believers, stretching her feeble hands between Peter and John and around James' feet, she made a final plunge and touched Jesus' garment. Matthew states that she touched the hem of his garment (Matt. 9:20). Healing was immediate. What medical science of the day could not accomplish for twelve years, the Ruler did in a moment when faith empowered belief.

A dramatic pause ensued. Jesus stopped abruptly, the noisy crowd looked on expectantly as Jesus asked, "Who touched me?" As all denied, Peter stepped forward with the obvious question, "Master, the crowds surround you and press in on you." But Jesus replied, "Someone touched me; for I noticed that power had gone out from me." Something extraordinary had happened, for virtue—in the original Greek, *dunamis* or power—had gone out from him.

Conceivably, Jesus must have said to Peter, "This is not the touch of a pressing crowd." This is a touch by "somebody" with intentionality, for it is deliberate, purposeful with expectancy, an expectancy that only genuine faith inspires. Virtue with transforming power responded that day when "somebody" rose above the curiosity of a motley throng and touched the Ruler. The transformation was immediate; the woman was healed, made whole in Matthew's account.

Becoming "somebody" in God's kingdom requires the touch of faith with an uncommon purpose, with intentionality that is unspoiled with doubt, a faith with a singleness of purpose, knowing that there is no other balm in Gilead. As Matthew records this miracle, he has the sick woman saying, "If I only touch his cloak, I will be made well" (Matt. 9:21). This is not perhaps or maybe, terms and attitudes that impede the instantaneity of miraculous accomplishments in our lives. Our perpetual cry should be, "Lord, I believe; help my unbelief."

This word "will" is material to the view of faith so critical to the immediacy of divine response in this story. The woman, who has now become "somebody" in stating that "I shall be made whole," expressed more than simple futurity. "Shall" in this context expressed emphatic intention, or rather, emphatic expectation. This is futurity with undiluted certainty. The desired effect preceded the act. The woman was healed internally and awaited only the physical manifestation. Expressing such undiluted, virtue-extracting faith is possible only as one is first touched by Jesus.

Blessings multiply when God's grace elicits from us a cry of hope, a touch of simple faith. First, we are separated from the curious throng, the motley crowd, the faceless mass of humanity and become "somebody." Second, should a faith with emphatic expectation match God's assessment of urgency, response is immediate. Response in this instance was immediate because circumstances demanded it. In the third place, wholeness in this instance means total transformation. Jesus said to the healed woman, "Take heart, daughter; your faith has made you well" (Matt. 9:22).

She came as a faceless, sick, unknown nobody; she left that scene physically healed, spiritually transformed, and a member in the family of God, for Jesus addressed her as "daughter." She is "somebody," a child of God because expectant faith and divine compassion transformed her that day on the way to Jairus' house. Jesus is still on the way of mercy; he is alert and awaiting the touch of human need. And he is never too busy for the single soul whose voice he recognizes among the clang and clatter of the curious throng. He was on a mission of service when he stopped to heal. And Jesus is no respecter of persons. A sick unknown woman is of the same standing as the daughter of a church officer.

Finally, access to Jesus needs no intermediary. The touch of faith is immediate. The sick woman did not need an appointment secretary in order to see Jesus. She did not ask Peter if she might see Jesus. There is only one mediator between God and the shackled soul, the man named Jesus.

The mad rush for a life of importance and meaning continues. The empty symbols of wealth, power, social standing, and celebrity status still carry the day as the final answers to the ultimate quest. Wealth, power, and social status all have relative value and are needed for transactional existence. But they can never provide answers regarding human finitude, which essentially is the basic human problem. Becoming somebody needs a transcendent source, and that source is Jesus. A seeking soul is bestowed significance when, responding to articulated and demonstrated faith, Jesus says, "Somebody has touched me."

Are you satisfied with your present status in life? Do you find the temptation to seek significance and meaning in the mundane overwhelming? There is a transforming answer in that "touch." Whom Jesus touches, he makes whole.

> *God of our salvation in whom we live, move, and have our being, direct us to the true source of a life of meaning with eternal consequences. Erase from our myopic vision those temporal and fugitive ambitions that, finally, are found wanting. Provide in all us that genuine faith that transforms our tentative touch of the Master into lifelong commitment. Amen.*

Nineteen

PROFILES OF PROPHETIC PREACHING

In those days John the Baptist appeared in the wilderness of Judea, proclaiming, 'Repent, for the kingdom of heaven has come near.' This is the one of whom the prophet Isaiah spoke when he said, 'The voice of one crying out in the wilderness: Prepare the way of the Lord, make his paths straight.

—Matthew 3:1–3

AMONG MASTER PREACHERS documented by sacred and secular sources, John the Baptist holds a unique place. He publicly launched Jesus' earthly ministry by baptizing him in the Jordan and announcing that he, John, was simply a preparer of the way of the Lord. Relinquishing any claim to fame for baptizing the Savior, John declared that he was unworthy even to bear the Savior's shoes. Such humility, when related to ministry, lays the foundation for greatness, for it recognizes the source of legitimacy and power. It follows that Jesus declares, "Truly I tell you, among those born of women no one has arisen greater than John the Baptist" (Matt. 11:11).

The ministry of John the Baptist epitomizes profiles in effective prophetic preaching, profiles that can inspire and inform aspirants to this highest of all callings. I shall discuss them under the rubrics of the man, the moment, the message, and the miracle.

The Man. Sent by no conference committee, without the imprimatur of the ecclesiastical authorities of the day, bereft of all the accoutrements possessed by well-financed evangelistic campaigns, equipped only with a sanctified voice, this strange man appeared in the wilderness of Judea preaching the gospel of repentance.

But who is this man dressed as a bushman, eating an unfamiliar fare—locust and honey from desert bees—looking like a modern beatnik, devoid of credentials from Ivy League seminaries of the day; on what grounds rests his prophetic legitimacy? John 1:6 gives the only necessary credentials for John's ministry. "There was a man sent from God, whose name was John." Intellectually prepared, he certainly was, for he quoted from scripture. But his call was divinely sanctioned, a necessary credential for all who dare wear the prophetic mantle.

The Moment. "In those days John the Baptist appeared in the wilderness of Judea, proclaiming . . ." (Matt. 3:1). Those days are referenced because relevance demands congruity between message and moment. While I was reading for the doctorate in Ethics and Society at the University of Chicago in the late sixties, civil rights activists among divinity students severely criticized the church as being an irrelevant institution because of its perceived unconcern for justice.

John came upon the scene in those days. Those were days of Roman rule and Jewish resentment. Roman soldiers harshly enforced taxation requirements even to the point of brutality. Fraud, violence, servitude, false accusation, blackmail, plunder, temple desecration by money-changers, perfunctory performance of priestly functions and immorality, including incest in the king's court, were frequent activities in Israel. John was later beheaded by Herod because he condemned Herod for living with Herodias, his brother's wife (Mark 6:16-28). Those days were a "moment" crying out for precise preaching.

The Message. In those days came John preaching. Effective preaching must be timely and relevant. It must speak to the times. Jesus instructed his disciples to know the signs of the times. Evil practices and downright sinful behavior ran the gamut of national life in John's day. His message was direct and uncompromising. "Repent, for the kingdom of heaven has come near" (Matt. 3:2).

What appears in this text is just the topical sentence in John's sermon. A piercing sermon speaks directly to people with specific needs. Pleasing generalities and eloquent phrases may attract large congregations but few converts. Preachers may be tempted to be popular rather than prophetic, a temptation occasioned by congregations seeking pastors preaching pabulum and not piercing truth.

The apostle Paul in writing to Timothy encourages him to preach the word and be mindful of those who seek to hear pleasantries, teachings that do not engage the conscience. "For the time is coming when people will not put up with sound doctrine, but having itching ears, they will accumulate for themselves teachers to suit their own desires . . ." (2 Tim. 4:3). The New English Bible gives a clearer rendition of this text. "For the time will come when they will not stand wholesome teaching, but will follow their own fancy and gather a crowd of teachers to tickle their ears."

The integrity of truth transcends human wants and speaks to human needs. Careful analysis of times, places, and people is critical if transformation of lives is expected. Preaching demands keen intellect informed by guided study of the Word, an understanding of personality dynamics, and cognizance of social trends. It is dishonoring to God and disrespectful of people for one to ascend the pulpit unprepared, claiming that the Spirit will provide instant insight and inspiration appropriate for the moment.

"Do your best to present yourself to God as one approved by him," says scripture (2 Tim. 2:15). Passion and emotion have their appropriate, indeed required, places in preaching. But passion without a principled postulate is pabulum. Decisions made under the intensity of heightened emotions tend to disappear in the heat of trials and tribulations. Proclamation of the truth must be done in "these days," when the church is challenged by the "acid of modernity."

The Miracle. "In those days" when John—the desert preacher, unknown by the intelligentsia, unpretentious as the priests, legitimately better lettered than the Sadducees, and more contemporary than the Pharisees in doctrine—called for repentance, he was intimately conversant with the times. He knew of sins in high places and throughout the nation; he knew of greed and oppression; he was fully aware of the meaningless rituals into which temple services had degenerated; he had studied the scriptures and had seen pharisaic righteousness for what it really was; he analyzed and saw the falsehood in scribal utterances of the day. As a student of scripture, John knew that in God's chronology of world events, a *kairos*, a signal juncture, a critical moment had arrived. So his message of repentance was to prepare the "way of the Lord." The time had come to announce the ministry of the Messiah, the world's Savior.

Response to this unconventional preacher was nothing short of a miracle. Speaking specifically to the sins of "those days" and the spiritual needs of his audience, crowds from Jerusalem and all Judea and surrounding regions flocked to hear him. They did not queue up to enter an air-conditioned, elegantly decorated hall; they did not board a bus or drive the latest automobile downtown to hear a well-known miracle worker. They streamed to the desert to hear a "voice" of legitimacy, a "voice" of credibility, the voice of the one crying in the wilderness "Repent, for the kingdom of heaven has come near."

Crowds responded, confessing their sins and receiving baptism. A ministry credentialed by God and knowledgeable of truth, that speaks to the conditions of the times and spiritual needs of individuals and that remains humble in spirit but full of the Spirit, will see souls saved and lives transformed and will become an instrument in building God's realm on earth.

One with heaven's credentials, speaking to the moment, thus delivering a relevant message and utilizing appropriate methods, will hear souls cry out, "What must we do to inherit eternal life?" The crowning reward for prophetic preaching is this question. In John's case, his apex in ministry was baptizing Jesus of Galilee. He, a desert preacher, launched the Christian era. Thank God for this "foolishness of preaching," for it is God's instrument to trumpet the gospel.

Every believer is a commissioned witness of the hope that saves. An ostentatious display of intellect, media gadgets, and wealth are not necessary for effective witnessing. Passion to share the good news will find an effective way.

In a world of broken relationships, injustice, suffering, and international conflicts, human beings need a message of hope, a message that convicts, converts, and transforms. The apostle Paul reminds us "God, by the foolishness of preaching," will "save them that believe." Send us, Oh God, preachers for these days who will trumpet the gospel of relevance. Amen.

PART FIVE

Triumph of Hope and Faith

Twenty

WHEN GOD SEEMS SILENT

I cry aloud to God, aloud to God, that he may
hear me. In the day of my trouble I seek the Lord;
in the night my hand is stretched out without wearying;
my soul refuses to be comforted. . . . Will the Lord
spurn forever, and never again be favorable? Has his
steadfast love ceased forever? Are his promises at an end
for all time? Has God forgotten to be gracious?
Has he in anger shut up his compassion?

—Psalm 77:1–2, 7–9

DOES THE TONE of complaint and seeming rejection in this text sound familiar? Are there times when a stream of depressing problems and perplexing questions brings you to a cul-de-sac in life's pilgrimage with no perceivable exit, no way out? And is faith placed under serious test when you are apt to ask "Where is God?"

A young man, as the story goes, faced the horror and tragedies of modern warfare. It was a day of modern life and modern war. A group of believers gathered in their little country church for worship. A bomber flying above released its agent of destruction upon the unwitting band of worshippers. Destruction was complete. Building and people were reduced to ashes. No doctors were called, for there were no available wounds to heal. Rescue squads were unnecessary, undertakers could perform no service, and there was no need for the clergy.

People from the little village gathered to view the carnage that war had brought to such a peaceful community. Tragedies do not discriminate, for even worshippers are not immune from the untrammeled forces of evil unleashed east of Eden. Questions of suffering goodness, though unuttered by most, overtook that crowd. One young man overwhelmed by this carnage uttered, as he turned to leave, "Where is God?" At such times God seems silent.

The character in the psalm, thought by some to be David, is often called the chief physician. His cry dramatizes a familiar paradox in human experience, skepticism and hope. This was a soul under great distress. Such words found in verse two—"In the day of my trouble I seek the Lord; in the night my hand is stretched out without wearying; my soul refuses to be comforted"—describe a wounded soul in despair. Although nonspecific regarding the exact nature of his trouble, David states, in the King James Version, "My sore ran in the night, and ceased not: my soul refused to be comforted."

These are wounds that cause agonizing pain, sometimes to the point of utter despair or hopelessness. Two aspects of this painful travail of the psalmist's experience identify the depth of his agony. First, the sore ran in the night. It seems that sickness intensifies at night. Darkness brings a sense of loneliness, a feeling of separation from friends, families, and immediate care. Whether literal or symbolic, separation from connectedness is a basic human fear. Loneliness, despite our increasingly populating world, represents a current dilemma. Listen to our senior citizens tucked away in some stuffy corner in a nursing home, undercared, unvisited, and often underfed. Hear the plaintive plea of a single mother struggling to provide shelter and clothing for her children as she labors for minimum pay at daytime and retires to relentless loneliness at night, knowing that recurring realities await her tomorrow. Yes, sores in the night mean intense agony, unbearable pain, a sense of helplessness.

In the King James Version of the text, the psalmist declares that his trouble, his "sore" did not only run at night, it "ceased not." This pain was not merely intense, it seemed endless. Certainly, while hours of bliss and joy, especially with loved ones, pass quickly, times of stress and pain seem like an eternity; they cease not, says the psalmist. Familiarity with expressed experiences in these verses elicits visceral responses in us. Who among us has not wallowed in the Slough of Despond? Who has not walked through that deep dark valley with no perceivable sunlight, no end in sight? Who has not felt dejected and alone at the most trying times along life's highway, when it seems there is no reason for living?

At such times, dejection seems final when calls for divine help, earnest prayers, go "unanswered." Then God seems silent. Then come the questions, "Have I not been a faithful follower, have I not been a regular church supporter, a friend and helper of the less fortunate?" The question of suffering goodness has engaged theologians and ethicists for ages. Essentially the question is, "How does a powerful sovereign God permit such evil, pain, and destruction on the earth over which God rules?" "Is God just an absentee landlord?" This problem of theodicy, or evil in a world ruled by an omnipotent God, becomes even more problematic for the one whose "sore" runs in the night. "Why me?" is often the question.

For the author of the text before us the silence of God presents soul-searching problems and questions: "I think of God, and I moan; I meditate, and my spirit faints." "Will the Lord spurn forever, and never again be favorable? Has his steadfast love ceased forever? Are his promises at an end for all time?" (verses 3–5). Coming from the author of this psalm, David, we believe, a man schooled in the tutelage of adversity and who had attained very close relationship with God, these questions possess profound implications. Here is a faithful man in deep distress, in what he calls his "day of trouble" calling desperately for help from the God he has served, but God seems silent.

Should he renounce his faith and revert to doubt and remorse? Should he call in question all the days of sacrifice and service? Should he succumb to reviling friends and subtle suggestions by the tempter of our souls? No. The mettle of meticulous faith triumphs. "My soul," says the psalmist, "refuses to be comforted." "I consider the days of old, and remember the years of long ago, I commune with my heart in the night; I meditate and search my spirit." "And I say, 'It is my grief that the right hand of the Most High has changed'" (verses 2, 5, 6, 10).

Here is mature, profound faith, "my soul refused to be comforted." There is no surrender here to self-pity and self-flagellation.

Rather there is a marked transition from grief and expostulation to hope and confidence. Experience and remembrance come into play here. The writer recalls the works of his God and the wonders of past times. He does not find fault with God, because he does not understand fully the workings of God. After a diligent search of heart, praise, gratitude, and adoration issue from his lips. For those who walk faithfully with God and who have come to know God will recall a continuous divine presence, even when God seems silent. Often we suffer from our own infirmities brought on by errant ways and blame the Almighty.

Does God always speak? I believe so. Then why seeming silence? God speaks to us through scripture, through nature, through profound exegetical preaching, and though the testimony of faithful followers. Our spirit in continual communion with our Maker receives, intuitively, guidance in times of need. At times the answer is not the expected, so there is divine "silence."

As I drove on one of the scenic back roads of America one day enjoying luxuriant mountain foliage, green grasslands, verdant valleys, and an occasional stream running down a hillside, I was listening to the most beautiful song being sung by my most favorite artist. The moment was superb and soothing. This must be a taste of utopia, I mused. Suddenly, the music waned, grating statics exuded from my expensive and never-before-poor-performance radio. The radio station must be at fault. Its poor transmission disturbed the tranquility and serenity of this splendid moment in time.

Potential causes of disruption in transmitting that soothing music never entered my mind, like distance from the radio station, the mountain range, competing frequencies, breakdown of the station, and, of course, my own radio seeing its last days. Subsequent examination disclosed that the only culprit in this breakdown of communication was my faulty radio. There was no problem at the source of transmission; the problem resided at the point of reception.

Communication with God involves a point of origin and a point of reception. The appropriate question is not whether God is speaking. Rather, it is whether or not we are listening, whether or not we are attuned to the frequency originating with our God. We hear that to which we are attuned. As the story goes, two men were debating the existence of God on a busy street in the city of New York. The unbeliever argued that no one can testify to the existence of God, for no one has seen God or heard God's voice. As the two argued at a very busy street corner at a peak hour when voices were loud and cars rushed by, the believer took a quarter from his pocket, tossed it in the air and it came crashing down on cemented sidewalk. The people stopped suddenly and voices subsided as all eyes focused on the sidewalk searching for the fallen quarter.

"There," said the believer, "people hear the sound of that to which they are attuned even when there are competing voices." Those attuned to God will hear God's voice among the bustle and clatter of discordant voices. So when every other voice is hushed and in quietude we wait before God, the silence of the soul makes more distinct the voice of God. No, our God is never silent.

Is your soul troubled by "unanswered" questions? Keep attuned by faith to the Source of truth, for "faith is the assurance of things hoped for, the conviction of things not seen" (Heb. 11:1).

Eternal Presence, open our eyes that we may see your uninterrupted acts of mercy in your world. Open our ears that we may hear your voice above discordant and conflicting signals trumpeted by a confused world. Grant us the capacity to wait upon you. Amen.

Twenty-One

SONGS IN THE NIGHT

I commune with my heart in the night;
I meditate and search my spirit.

—Psalm 77:6

I call to remembrance my song in the night:
I commune with mine own heart; and my spirit
made diligent search

—Psalm 77:6 KJV

LIFE IS A MOSAIC of light and shadows. Its pilgrimage traverses highways strewn with long stretches of paved paths, scenic countrysides, green grasslands, shady dales, and sunlit mountains. But it also takes us through rocky roads, dangerous curves, drought-stricken terrains, and mountains that seem impossible to climb. Life experiences are mostly triumphs but our journey also encounters tragedies, disappointments, failures, and despair, defined as shadows.

We are reminded that nature is both cruel and kind. Nature is waterfalls, placid lagoons, white sand beaches, luxuriant rain forests, chirping birds, and refreshing altruism among human beings. Nature is also earthquakes, tornadoes, earth-parching droughts, man-eating tigers, still births, and destructive actions among humans. This mosaic of light and shadows is the substance of life this side of Eden.

It is easy to be ecstatic, jubilant, and full of praise when life's way brings fulfilled desires, realized dreams, physical well-being, and every conceivable blessing for which the soul seeks. The test of faithful following resides in responses to tragedies and failures along life's way. As a fourth grader, I heard the following quatrain with its simple message that has been a resource to me through the years: "It is easy enough to be pleasant when life rolls along like a song. But the one worthwhile is the one who can smile when everything goes dead wrong."[16] The question posed by this perplexing paradox pertaining to life is "Are there reservoirs of spiritual maturity and faith on which the perplexed soul may be enabled to sing songs in the night?"

David, to whom Psalm 77 is attributed, says "In the day of my trouble I sought the Lord: my sore ran in the night, and ceased not: my soul refused to be comforted" (Ps. 77:2 KJV). The text does not expand on David's plight. It bespeaks a man in the depths of despair. His was a life of triumphs and tragedies. A king in his youth, a brilliant and effective ruler in Israel, a defiant and successful warrior against enemies of Israel, a planner of the temple in Jerusalem, though he was not permitted to build it, he was indeed a faithful servant of God, a friend of God.

But David experienced trouncing tragedies. His triumph over the Philistines's giant Goliath earned him King Saul's jealous rage. His life was in danger as Saul pursued him from cave to cave throughout the land. His adulterous relationship with Bathsheba, Uriah's wife; the incestuous activity between Ammon, David's son, and his sister Tamar; Absalom's murder of Ammon for violating their sister, and Absalom's rebellion against his father, David, seeking to wrest away the throne—all these were tragedies in his life. This conspiracy by Absalom and his death in battle brought sorrow and great pain to King David, who mourned profoundly for his son (2 Sam. 18:33). These low, painful moments in David's life we construe to be "night sores" that pained, putrefied, and festered in seeming endlessness.

The word "night" in our text may be applied both literally and metaphorically. Some scholars use it literally. Accordingly, "my sore ran in the night" and "I call to remembrance my song in the night" mean that the author, identified as a musician, constructed his songs literally at nighttime. But the metaphorical application of "sore" and "night" electrifies, enlivens, and endows this passage with meaning touching universal human experience.

Who has not had his/her slough of despond? Who has not felt a loneliness almost comparable to death? Who has not lost a very dear friend that left an emptiness without remedy? Who has not stood by the last resting place of a relative, a family member, and walked away facing an eternity of separation? Indeed, the world is replete with those who walk the deprived paths of paucity and dire need, attend the university of adversity, fall victims of the perils of plenty, are tainted with passions of pride, and live each day without hope of a better tomorrow. In David's words, these represent sores that run in the night and cease not. They cease not because no end is seen; tomorrow replicates today.

What does God expect of the faithful in these "nights" of trouble, depths of despair, feelings of failure? David called to remembrance his "song in the night." Literal or metaphorical, testimonies of praise or lyrics in melody, those songs brought some degree of relief to David as well as praise to God. They recalled past years, "days of old," and "the years of long ago." Songs in the night are songs of experience issuing from the crucible of trials with a mixture, at times, of triumph and tragedy. In spite of David's trouble (verse 2), he sings, "I will call to mind the deeds of the Lord; I will remember your wonders of old" (verse 11).

Melodies of praise and exultation exuding from catastrophic misfortunes leave indelible imprints on others, as well as generate profound resolve in those singing songs of victory. No one in recorded history, sacred or secular, has been as lifted up as a model of faithful following under the most extreme affliction as has Job. For no apparent reason known to him, he was ravaged physically, domestically, economically, and socially. Covered with burning repulsive sores, encouraged by his wife to "Curse God, and die," suffering the loss of his sons and daughters, enduring the loss of his immense wealth, and tormented by his three friends with the charge that his affliction was the result of sins in his life, Job lamented the day of his birth. All reasons to live seemed to have vanished.

From such a "night" of absolute distress comes the crowning benediction any soul can receive, "In all this Job did not sin or charge God with wrong-doing" (Job 1:22). And his song of praise is punctuated by worshiping God and declaring, "Though he slay me, yet will I trust in him" (Job 13:15 KJV). Throughout the ages, such sustained faith under the most inhumane circumstances and excruciating pain has brought courage to struggling souls and resolve to the tempted. God rewarded Job copiously in his later days far beyond the blessings and possessions he experienced prior to his trials.

Some of the masterpieces in literature, art, and music, and other notable achievements came out of severe physical defects or some low moments in human life. Out of John Milton's blindness came *Paradise Lost;* John Bunyan's imprisonment produced *Pilgrims Progress;* Michaelangelo's *Last Judgment* received its finishing touches when the artist was almost blind. Charles Spurgeon, one of the world's great preachers, suffered excruciating rheumatic pains that caused periodic interruptions of his ministry. Paul, the theologian of the New Testament, declared an unspecified affliction that did not hinder his brilliant and most effective ministry. Martin Luther King Jr.'s "I Have A Dream" speech that has impacted so many lives worldwide, a speech comprehensive in content and brilliant in style and delivery, came out of the "night" of race prejudice and brokenness in human relations, a "night" that eventually cost him his life.

Paraphrasing a poet's perception of the quality of the testimonies issuing from the crucible of experience, I recall this profound statement: "We look before and after, and pine for what is not. Our sincerest laughter with some pain is fraught. Our sweetest songs are those that tell of saddest thought."[17] We must find time for the pain, for it is the stuff of which life is made.

An authoritative, authenticating, affirming voice rises from the vortex of experience. It is a voice of discipline and perseverance. It is necessary to create and test the mettle of faith, for without faith it is impossible to please God.

As one story goes, a man found a cocoon of a butterfly. One day he watched carefully for hours as the emerging butterfly struggled to force its way through a small opening in the cocoon. Assuming that it was making no progress in unraveling itself and being willing to help, the man, thinking that the butterfly was about to give up the struggle, used a pair of scissors to snip off the rest of the cocoon, permitting the butterfly to emerge easily without great effort. It was left with a swollen body and small, shriveled wings. The man waited for normalcy, for fully developed wings that would support a body easily in flight. But he waited in vain. The body did not shrink and the wings remained weak and shriveled. That butterfly never flew; it spent the rest of its life crawling around with undeveloped wings and a bloated body. In his willingness to help, the man circumvented God's way for the normal development of a butterfly. Struggling to emerge from a cocoon is required to remove fluid from a butterfly's body and strengthen its wings to initiate normal life with its myriad challenges.

Indeed, the way of the cross leads home. It was a lonely and painful "night" for our Savior as he was dragged, ridiculed, reviled, and rejected on the way to the cross. The lonely depths of his agony cry out, "My Father, if it is possible, let this cup pass from me; yet not what I want but what you want" (Matt. 26:39). Our hope, our salvation resides in that sacrifice, for out of that "night" comes the most significant melody streaming down from Golgotha's height, "Father," said Jesus, "forgive them; for they do not know what they are doing" (Luke 23:34).

Were you there when they crucified my Lord? I was, for his victory through suffering has provided me a "balm in Gilead to make the wounded whole," and when "sometimes I feel discouraged and think my work's in vain, but then the Holy revives my soul again." When the inevitable comes and casts a shadow of doubt, when the pain of failure and loss seems unbearable, when the dark night of rejection and loneliness descends like a cloud upon your soul, sing a song of worship, a testimony of victory, for there is no melody equal to songs in the night.

In shady, green pastures, so rich and so sweet,
God leads His dear children along;
Where the water's cool flow bathes the weary one's feet,
God leads His dear children along.
Sometimes on the mount where the sun shines so bright,
God leads His dear children along;
Sometimes in the valley, in darkest of night,
God leads His dear children along.
Tho sorrows befall us and Satan oppose,
God leads his dear children along;
Thru grace we can conquer, defeat all our foes,

God leads His dear children along.
Away from the mire and away from the clay,
God leads His dear children along;
Away up in glory, eternity's day,
God leads His dear children along.
Some thru the waters, some thru the flood,
Some thru the fire, but all thru the blood;
Some thru great sorrow, but God gives a song,
In the night season and all the day long."[18]

Twenty-Two

AN AMBIVALENT JOURNEY

Read Luke 15:11–32

HUMANITY'S GREATEST ASSET is also their most potential liability, and that is their God-given freedom of choice. Were humans robots, decisions would be preprogrammed and predictable. But then human beings would be machines driven by paper plans and buttons. There would be no opportunity for psychological maturity and intellectual development. Management would be easy, but leadership would be unnecessary, for leadership requires voluntary following. Robots are managed, not led.

With relentless ease we misuse our freedom to choose, often with dire consequences. Temptations to make poor choices multiply—especially among young people. As a boy of seventeen, I fell victim to that freedom and had to pay an unforgettable price. An Indian wedding, with its most spectacular rituals, was happening about two miles from my home. Without seeking my parents' consent, I attended the wedding, stayed all night, and returned home the following morning with great trepidation, for this was a first in my experience.

The consequence of my choice did not bring the expected corporal punishment, which my father was not reticent in administering even at my age of seventeen. Instead, he had me walk with him for about twenty miles over some of Jamaica's most hilly terrain to keep an appointment. Effects consequential to a night without sleep were more excruciating than a flogging, which would have lasted for a much shorter period. Choices do have consequences, and wrong choices often yield dire consequences.

"An Ambivalent Journey," which is the title of this sermon, examines the ambiguous decision of a young man who had dreams of grandeur to be financed by means that he had not earned. He took a journey to places he had not known and consorted with frivolous persons who turned out to be fair-weather friends. Consequences of this ambivalent journey continue to invite critical examination of choices, for they inevitably lead to pleasure or pain, triumph or tragedy.

The fifteenth chapter of Luke records three parables that Jesus spoke in response to his detractors' criticism that he was associating with sinners. The third parable begins with verse 21. Usually called the parable of the prodigal son, it relates the story of a man with two sons, the younger of whom asked for his portion of his father's possessions that would be willed to him. Upon receiving his portion, the young man hastily left home for a distant country where he easily made "friends" and enjoyed a wild life of licentious and recklessly extravagant spending.

Soon, he and his money separated and he became penniless. Deserted by his fair-weather friends, he ended up feeding swine and often shared their meals. Recalling the opulence of his past, he was now faced with another choice. Should he return to his father, seek forgiveness, and desire to be a hired servant? Or should he remain in a swine pit and waste away in need, self-pity, and sin?

He chose wisely this time. He arose from the pit, the pit of swine, hunger, forgetfulness, and self-pity, and journeyed back home. But the waiting father, who longed for his return, and from whose heart the son had never really left home, saw him from a distance through the microscopic love of a forgiving father. "Forget that speech about being hired as a servant. Here is the ring for your finger signifying reentry to your father's house," said his father.

Two decisions: one to leave; the other to return. One caused painful consequences; the other evoked forgiveness and reestablishment of a favored position and privilege in the household.

Culling some valuable lessons from this parable of prodigality, we discover some telling traits that seem to be precursors of poor decision making:

The young man was presumptuous and premature in his request. Bequests are made and are not earned. To request an inheritance is presumptuous. Further, it is usually made after the death of the testator.

He was in a desperate hurry. Shortly after receiving his goods he left home (Luke 15:13). Decisions made hurriedly are usually wrong and counterproductive. Perhaps he was at the age of restlessness and was bored by the rules and recurring monotony of home life. He sought adventure and experience because home rules were just too strict. Does this sound familiar?

He was a poor economist. He took all the funds his father had given him. And, if one takes it all, one will spend it all. Taking it all might have meant a clean break from home with no plans to return (verse 13).

He was in quest of anonymity; he went to a far country. Distance meant disconnection from home. Anonymity provided freedom from constraints, absence of rules, low expectations. Freedom without rules and expectations, especially for the uninitiated, the young, becomes a recipe for disaster. Some people need to escape from freedom, and thus escape from self-destruction.

The young man was a spendthrift. He led an extravagant lifestyle in that far country that left him penniless. The text says that he engaged in riotous living (verse 13). He became the new man in town with a lot of cash, and willing to entertain lavishly. Waste, exuberance, conspicuous consumption, and self-gratification defined his way of life in a far country. He wanted it all, and he wanted it now. Does this sound familiar? Nineteen hundred years ago, this young man was the model of the modern youth. Instant gratification characterizes our age. Oh, he took it all, and he spent it all (verse 14).

After losing money and friends, he was given the most despicable job in town, a feeder of swine. If he were a Jew, this job made him almost an outcast, for swine were deemed unclean animals in that society. His fair-weather friends disappeared when his funds dried up. The unkindest cut of all is the stab of neglect and the lash of disdain by those who feed at the trough of one's plenty and who forget when one is in dire need. Mr. Man-about-Town became an unknown feeder of swine, hungry and broke, for no one gave him anything (verse 16).

A series of bad choices placed this prodigal on a slippery slope, a downhill slide that took him to the bottom of the socioeconomic ladder. His request was premature, he took all his cash, chose the wrong country (lost all connections), chose the wrong friends, engaged in extravagant life style, and lost it all. And freedom ends when options run out.

Redemptively, he had another choice, for this parable is describing the ultimate goal of salvation, and that is to reach to the deepest dungeon of degradation to snatch souls shackled by sin and circumstances and give them hope and wholesome relationship with God. The text says, "I will get up and go to my father, and I will say to him, 'Father, I have sinned against heaven and before you'" (verse 18).

He came to his senses and realized his mistakes, recalling that life is a million times better at home than in the far country. He assumed the posture of penitence; he sought forgiveness; he went home to a waiting father, who reestablished his status as a son. It was an ambivalent journey with all the elements of doubt and boldness, wrong choices and the choice that brought hope.

There is glorious relevance in the parable of the prodigal for every thinking soul. Profound in its simplicity and subtle in its plasticity, the theme of choice and forgiveness running through this telling story tends to escape those who perceive it as directed at young people only. Its critical emphasis on choices accentuates a most human activity in which we engage continually. And choices determine destiny. Our choices produce either success or failure, but all choices determine consequences.

Thanks be to our waiting heavenly Father, whose hands are never too short to reach that soul that comes to him/herself in the pit of life. Comforting it is to say with the psalmist: "If I take the wings of the morning and settle at the farthest limits of the sea, even there your hand shall lead me, and your right hand hold me fast" (Psalm 139:9–10).

Isn't it sobering to be reminded that every choice has consequences? But it is very comforting to know that God's love extends to the depraved depths of human experience, to lift the fallen to a place of favor and forgiveness.

Father, forgive us for all indiscriminate decisions made in haste without the wisdom of heaven. Create within us the desire and the capacity to know and understand thy will, and endow us with the courage to choose wisely with the resolve to obey always thy declared will. Amen.

Twenty-Three

TRIUMPHS AND TRAGEDIES
OF UNREALIZED POTENTIALS

And the Lord said, "Look, they are one people,
and they have all one language; and this is only the
beginning of what they will do; nothing that they
propose to do will now be impossible for them."

—**Genesis 11:6**

What are human beings that you are mindful of them,
mortals that you care for them? Yet you have made them
a little lower than God, and crowned them with glory and
honor. You have given them dominion over the works
of your hands; you have put all things under their feet.

—**Psalm 8:4–6**

See, this alone I found, that God made human beings
straightforward, but they have devised many schemes.

—**Ecclesiastes 7:29**

THESE SCRIPTURAL REFERENCES document divinely endowed resources humans may rely upon in life's myriad situations. Genesis
records the scheme conceived by the survivors of the flood, which involved the building of a tower tall enough to defy the onslaught of
another flood. So successful was their architectural design and con-

struction skills that God had to intervene by making it impossible for them to communicate. In aborting this project, which ran counter to the divine plan to save humanity, God paid compliments to the resources and potentials with which humankind is invested: "Nothing that they propose to do will now be impossible for them." The Contemporary English Version renders this passage: "This is just the beginning. Soon they will be able to do anything they want."

The eighth book of the Psalms further elevates humanity's seemingly limitless potential by declaring that human beings were made a little lower than God (Ps. 8:5) and that all things in nature had been placed under humanity's dominion.

Whereas the Genesis scripture documents human beings' power to do, to accomplish anything conceived, and Psalm 8 declares our authority to rule, the Ecclesiastes verse states our potential "to be." Human beings were created straightforward, or upright in the King James Version, but had devised many schemes, or sought out many inventions (KJV). To be upright connotes "to be right," to be moral. Inventions mean "to contrive," "to devise," "to invent." Moral uprightness is a goal of creation, which man's devices and contrivances have impeded.

Here are human beings in three dimensions endowed by the creator. Professionally, they can do anything they want (Genesis). Politically, they have been assigned dominion over the earth (Psalms). Morally, they were made upright, given a pristine beginning (Ecclesiastes). And although humanly devised schemes and moral lapses have somewhat diminished our abilities to make appropriate choices, God preserves these endowments and abilities. With God's help, we can realize the achievements for which we were created. It is indeed a social tragedy when our potentials go unrealized.

A young man I know is the oldest of seven siblings. As the first boy in that family, he is revered and expected to be a model of success for his siblings. Academically, he possesses the greatest potential, documented by high-school transcripts. With extreme sacrifices, because he is from a family of very modest means, he was sent to college.

But college life did not reflect his potentials. Social activities, marginal attention to academic requirements, and eventually a run-in with the law truncated college life. Abuse of alcohol and drugs has destroyed his health, and while he earns a few dollars as a blue-collar airport employee, he drifts, periodically, to his eighty-six-year-old mother's house for a meal provided by her small social security check. This is a true story with which I am very familiar. Here is a young man clearly endowed with mental resources to achieve whatever professional goals chosen, but he has wasted time, talent, and body temple and now subsists on the margin of an unfulfilled life. To his family, this is an agonizing tragedy of unrealized potentials. And to God, this is like seeds fallen on untilled soil. This life, so far, is a professional and moral failure.

The case of King Hezekiah of Judah represented potential tragedy for his entire kingdom. Threatened with an attack by the nation of Assyria, King Hezekiah, in great fear, earnestly sought deliverance by God through Isaiah, the prophet. Standing before Isaiah, Hezekiah's messengers declared: "Thus says Hezekiah, This day is a day of distress, of rebuke, and of disgrace; children have come to the birth, and there is no strength to bring them forth" (2 Kings 19:3).

This passage is even more dramatically rendered in the Contemporary English Version: "These are difficult and disgraceful times. Our nation is like a woman too weak to give birth. Please pray for us who are left alive." Could Hezekiah be saying that this nation of Judah for whom God performed such mighty acts cannot now defend itself? The crisis facing King Hezekiah and Judah was serious, for their enemy, the Assyrians, had conquered most of Judah and now threatened to attack Jerusalem, the capital.

King Hezekiah had legitimate reasons to appeal to God for deliverance, for he was a God-fearing king. Scripture applauds his twenty-nine-year reign stating that, "he did what was right in the sight of the Lord just as his ancestor David had done" (2 Kings 18:3).

Hezekiah initiated unparalleled reform in Judah. In restoring the worship of Jehovah in Judah he accomplished more than any king before or after him. He actually destroyed heathen worship in the kingdom and resisted assaults by hostile nations.

The fourteenth year of his reign brought great threats and distress to the nation. King Sennacherib of Assyria became a formidable enemy. Having conquered Samaria ten years before and having pulverized other nations, Sennacherib was now determined to attack Jerusalem. Boasting of his conquests of nations, whose gods could not withstand his assaults, he warned Hezekiah that his God was helpless to deliver him.

At this distressing juncture, Hezekiah went to the house of God, assumed the posture of mourning, and sent emissaries to the prophet Isaiah seeking divine deliverance. Dramatizing the gravity of the Assyrian threat, Hezekiah through his emissaries declared that "children have come to the birth, and there is no strength to bring them forth" (2 Kings 19:3). Indeed, the peril of national defeat was imminent. The capital city of Jerusalem was all that was left of the nation of Judah, and Hezekiah beseeched Isaiah, "therefore lift up your prayer for the remnant that is left" (verse 4).

Only divine intervention could prevent defeat, for the weakened nation of Judah was depicted as a woman too weak to give birth. Giving birth is natural; it's a built-in potential of healthy women. A condition that hinders delivery of a child is an unspeakable tragedy, a tragedy of unrealized potential. Israel possessed all the resources necessary to become a great nation but squandered its potential, resulting in national decline.

Hezekiah and his kingdom had just one hope. God, who is the source of all life and whom Hezekiah had served faithfully as king for twenty-nine years, would not leave his faithful servant to be destroyed by the enemy.

Isaiah's prophetic utterances and Hezekiah's fervent prayer brought deliverance to Judah and destruction to the armies of Sennacherib. For God declared that the king of Assyria "shall not come into this city, shoot an arrow there, come before it with a shield . . ." (verse 32). As promised, God's words took effect that very night when an angel of God killed 185,000 Assyrian soldiers.

Weakened though we may be by the battering of life, when noble goals seem unachievable, when God-given potential falters before the enemies of our souls, there is the God of Hezekiah; there is our God, who can remove mountains and rekindle faltering faith.

So many talents are wasted on unworthy causes. Modest accomplishments are outcomes of modest expectations. God expects accomplishments of grandeur from those made in God's image.

Our opening texts describe human potential for greatness professionally, politically, and morally. Faithful adherence to God's plan will eventually render achievement of our manifest destiny. For greater is the God that is in us than the evil that is in the world. With God, hope is alive, victory is assured, and life is fulfilled. Glory! Alleluia!

Creator of every good and perfect gift, thank you for the numerous capacities and resources given us to achieve lofty goals. Keep before us always your expectations for our lives, and inspire us to accomplish our highest potential. Amen.

Twenty-Four

GLORY OF THE FINISHED TASK
Eden Restored

*But they have conquered him by the blood of the
Lamb and by the word of their testimony, for they did
not cling to life even in the face of death.*

—Revelations 12:11

THIS BOOK OF SPIRITUAL REFLECTIONS represents a journey of hope fueled by faith. It has been a checkered journey, begun in disobedience, strewn with triumphs and tragedies, punctuated with failures and penitence, spiritual deviancy and repentance. But it is a journey called Repentant Following, for it resembles an undulating terrain with peaks of elation and valleys of despair, sun-lit mountains with victory over evil and fog-filled vales when evil seems to prevail.

But hope never falters, for it is sustained by the promise in Eden, "I will put enmity between you and the woman, and between your offspring and hers; he will strike your head, and you will strike his heel" (Gen. 3:15).

In this prophetic utterance, God declares to the evil one that there will be enmity, conflict between his followers, the children of evil, and the seed of the woman, who are the children of light. I believe that the followers of the evil one include those who persecuted Christians in centuries past. It is a conflict that has bruised the seed of the woman, a feud that put Jesus on the cross. But it will ultimately bring about the destruction of Satan and evil; then will his head be bruised.

It is conceivably more lethal to wound one's head than one's heel. Final destruction, total eradication of evil from the earth, and ultimate deliverance for the faithful constitute the kernel of our faith.

John, author of the Book of Revelation, while in exile on the island of Patmos, was shown glimpses of the Christian Church leading up to the last days. And John claims critical urgency for his message, declaring, "for the time is near" (Rev. 1:3).

John, in his vision, was instructed to write to the seven churches in Asia (Rev. 1:11). Each church, although geographically located in Asia, seems to possess certain characteristics of God's church in different periods of its history. The church at Ephesus, though impatient with evil and hypocrisy, has lost its first love (Rev. 2:2–4). To the faithful is the promise "to eat from the tree of life that is in the paradise of God." This sounds like paradise restored.

The church of Smyrna will experience great tribulation and persecution but is encouraged to overcome. The church at Pergamos exists in the midst of evil (Satan's seat) and is accused of teaching false doctrine (verse 14). And the church is exhorted to repent. The church of Thyatira is accommodating to idol worship and fornication. Although retribution is promised the unfaithful, those that overcome will be made rulers over nations.

The church at Sardis has not lived up to its good name, and judgment will be meted out unexpectedly. But there is hope for Sardis. There were believers there who kept the faith.

Upon the church at Philodelphia a benediction of praise was invoked, because they obeyed God's Word and did not deny God's name. Before them a door of opportunity was opened, and the overcomer will be made a pillar in God's temple. Laodicea, the seventh church, received a most scathing rebuke: "I know your works; you are neither cold nor hot. I wish that you were either cold or hot. So, because you are lukewarm, and neither cold nor hot, I am about to spit you out of my mouth" (Rev. 3:15, 16).

To be lukewarm bespeaks a state of neutrality, of mediocrity, which is a precondition to spiritual atrophy. In this state, believers are lulled into self-imposed tranquility, anesthetized, as it were, by feelings of spiritual superiority; this loss of religious zeal and momentum elicits a most scathing rebuke: "For you say, 'I am rich, I have prospered, and I need nothing.' You do not realize that you are wretched, pitiable, poor, blind, and naked" (Rev. 3:17).

Despite this miserable state of the Laodicean church, God's love and forgiveness bring hope: "I reprove and discipline those whom I love. Be earnest, therefore, and repent" (verse 19). The gospel of hope, like a golden thread, runs through the sermons in this book. Repentant following is the only way; it is the way of the cross, and as the song says, "The way of the cross leads home."

These seven churches of Asia depict the titanic struggles between the forces of good and evil that began in Eden. Across centuries of tribulations and persecution, God has had a faithful few carrying the banner of truth. And they were not perfect followers, for even Abraham, while in Egypt, told a half a truth, which amounts to a whole lie when he told Pharaoh that Sarai was his sister. Indeed, she was his sister, but she was also his wife. The Bible is fair and objective in describing humanity. It speaks of evil in the faithful, and good in the unfaithful. It tells of David's crime and adultery involving Uriah and Bathsheba, but it describes David's reign as a reign of God's servant David (1 Chron. 17:4).

Similar challenges of triumphs and tragedies, faithful following and moral lapses engaged these seven churches of Asia. The Book of Revelation describes, with its eschatological emphasis, world-shaking events leading to the restoration of Eden. It depicts the final struggle between the seed of the woman (God's Church) and the serpent, the devil.

But the Lamb of God will overcome the evil one. Bruised by Jesus' heels at the cross, and his death knell tolled by Jesus' resurrection, Satan will be ultimately destroyed, with his host of followers. Then, the author of Revelation writes, "The kingdom of the world has become the kingdom of our Lord and of his Messiah, and he will reign forever and ever" (Rev. 11:15).

In this realm, former things such as pain, tears, sorrow, and death will be gone forever. The Redeemer promises that all things will be made "new." Social dislocations and disobedience that caused the loss of Eden will be replaced by social harmony and obedience. Eden will be restored. Our earthly pilgrimage takes us from paradise lost to paradise restored.

To the repentant follower, victory is assured. Victory is promised by the way of the cross: "But they have conquered him by the blood of the Lamb and by the word of their testimony, for they did not cling to life even in the face of death" (Rev. 12:11).

Glorious are the prospects of Eden restored—harmony between humankind and God restored, for the saints will worship the Lamb continually, "day and night." Deceit and deception among the saved will disappear: "And in their mouth no lie was found; they are blameless" (Rev. 14:5). This depicts a state of social harmony. The lion and the lamb will lie down together, depicting a state of harmony in nature.

And a river runs through the city called the river of life. The tree of life, whose leaves are for the "healing of the nations" is found on the banks of the river of life. These are symbols of spiritual vitality, sustained zeal in contradistinction to the lukewarmness of Laodicea.

The saved will sing a new song (Rev. 14:3). It will be a song of victory forged by experience. They have been redeemed; they have been battered and bruised by persecutors. Angels cannot sing that song, for they have not experienced a victorious faith spawned by the crucible of tribulations.

Some may perceive this final resolution of the human condition utopian. Others may sink into the skeptic's mode of doubt and uncertainty regarding life's ultimate question. "This is it," they would say, "so eat, drink, and be merry, for death ends it all."

But utopian or skeptic, all face the sobering reality of our mortality, death.

If this is life's final answer to the agelong human quest for immortality, both the utopian and skeptic have valid views.

However, there prevails another view predicated on faith. It is a faith deeply embedded in scripture as the Apostle Paul states it: "The last enemy to be destroyed is death" (1 Cor. 15:26). The King James Version states it more prescriptively: "The last enemy that shall be destroyed is death."

Implied here is that death is not the final chapter in the lives of those who believe. For, like a golden thread running through each sermon in this book is the notion that we are saved by hope.

The call for repentance rings with a sense of urgency. "Listen! I am standing at the door, knocking," says the Ruler. "If you hear my voice and open the door, I will come in to you and eat with you, and you with me" (Rev. 3:20). This invitation is extended to the repentant follower as well as to those who have never believed. Opportunity knocks, and time is fleeting.

Here the prospects are triumphantly promising. The pristine beauty and cosmic harmony descriptive of Eden are restored. Broken relationships are made whole. The Creator and the Creator's creation achieve eschatological synthesis. Nature is now kind as the lion and the lamb "lie down together." Life "East of Eden" with all its physical, social, economic, and spiritual pathologies is replaced. And humans are invited to embrace this new life.

Jesus, the Alpha and Omega, promises to give freely the water of life to those who overcome. So the invitation comes to join the redeemed in proclaiming God King of Kings, and Lord of Lords. For worthy is our God to receive honor and glory, and power and praise.

Our Creator and Redeemer, praise, honor, and glory be to your name for this pleasing promise of Eden restored. Believers across the centuries have prayed for it. Prophets predicted it. Preachers proclaimed it, and Jesus died to restore it. Until then, we live with the consequences of the disharmonies that exist east of Eden. Preserve our faith that reminds us that behind the social pathologies of broken human relations, behind the play and interplay of national strife, stands God almighty, watching over us all. Amen.

NOTES

1. Reinhold Niebuhr, *The Nature and Destiny of Man,* vol. 1 (New York: Charles Scribner's Sons, 1947).

2. St. Augustine, *The City of God,* bk. XIX, chap.viii.

3. Lawrence Manson, ed., *The Tragedy of Julius Caesar* (New Haven: Yale University Press, 1957), 79.

4. H. Richard Niebuhr, *The Social Services of Denominationalism* (New York: World Publishing, 1929).

5. H. Richard Niebuhr, *The Kingdom of God in America* (New York: Harper, 1959).

6. James Rowe, "Love Lifted Me," 1912.

7. Ellen G. White, *Education* (Mountain View, Calif.: Pacific Publishing, 1903), 57.

8. William P. Merrill, "Rise Up, Oh Men of God!" 1911.

9. Harriet Eugenia Peck Buell, "A Child of the King," 1877; "My Father is Rich in Houses and Land" © 1941, General Conference of Seventh-day Adventists.

10. William Barclay, *More New Testament Words* (New York: Harper and Brothers, 1958). 11.

11. Ibid., 14.

12. Fanny J. Crosby, "Redeemed How I Love to Proclaim It," 1882.

13. Clara H. Scott, " Open My Eyes, That I May See," 1895.

14. Tucker Brooke and Jack Crawford, eds. *The Tragedy of Hamlet Prince of Denmark* (New Haven, Conn.: Yale University Press, 1954), 80–81.

15. Billy Graham, *Peace with God* (Garden City, N.Y.: Doubleday, 1956), 80.

16. Attributed to Ella Wheeler Wilcox, 1850–1919, U.S. writer, poet, and journalist in Allen Klein, *Quotations to Cheer You Up When the World Is Getting You Down* (New York: Sterling, 1991).

17. From Percy Bysshe Shelley (1792–1822), "To a Skylark."

18. George A. Young, "God Leads His Dear Children Along," 1903.